Anxiety Attacks
the Enemy Within

by

KARL WILLIAM MARX

authorHOUSE®

AuthorHouse™
1663 Liberty Drive, Suite 200
Bloomington, IN 47403
www.authorhouse.com
Phone: 1-800-839-8640

First published by AuthorHouse 7/18/2007

ISBN: 978-1-4343-1511-3 (sc)

Printed in the United States of America
Bloomington, Indiana

This book is printed on acid-free paper.

Dedication

This book is dedicated to each and every individual World Wide, who has the unpleasant experience of Anxiety and or Panic Attacks. May you ALL be relieved from this misfortune. Also I dedicate this book to my darling wife Kathy my little "Mud Bug" who encourages me to be what God intended me to be, and since I forgot to name my son Morgan in my last book, I acknowledge him in this one. God Bless you all. I also wish to plug my friends at Gospel Martial Arts Union, Johnny Russell, Mike McGee of Gospel Martial Arts Foundation, as well as Karate for Christ founded by Mike Crain who inspired me into the ministry. Mike Mc Gann a long time friend and former student. Also my friend Papa San from WOMA I can't name all the one's I want to but you know God knows who you are. However I can not again forget my great devoted students who did all my typing for me Matt Hickman who typed my first Book "Martial Arts Spirit," his brother Josh who helped him on my second book "If I Can Do It Anyone Can" and my last two books I am so grateful to Steven Miller. I appreciate and love you all. My son Victor Marx I pray God will bless your wonderful ministry "All Things Possible Ministries" And of course besides my 10 children, my love to my 14 Grand Children. God is so good and faithful.

Contents

Forward

When Soke Karl W. Marx, Sr., asked me to write something for his new book, I had a rush of different thoughts and feelings come over me. At first, I was humbled that he'd ask "little ole' me" to do such a thing. After all, who am I to be asked to add something to his latest work? Then I wondered what I could say that would be of value to the book, value to the reader and value to him to show him the respect and honor he so richly deserves. Among the other things I thought of, I believed it best to share something from the heart about his other books.

I found Soke Marx's book, "Martial Arts Spirit" via a search on Amazon.com. I was searching for books to help me with a number of things, among which was where being a Christian and martial artist came together. I was at a crucial time in my life that needed that information. Little did I know how much I'd learn about various types of attacks that we humans go through on a daily basis, often not realizing the results of those attacks. After reading that book, I went on a search for contact information for Soke on the Internet, because I simply felt compelled to let him know how much I enjoyed that book and how much it had helped me. Imagine how surprised I was when I was actually able to find his website and email address in the process. Even more surprising was that he actually answered me back wanting to know more about me and also saying, "God had you get in contact with me for a reason!" Boy, was he ever right on that one! The things I could tell you that have changed for me. But, that's really outside of the scope of what I'm writing here.

My many emails and occasional phone conversations with Soke Marx got me more interested in him as a person and so I ended up reading his book, "If I Can Do It, Anyone Can." What an interesting and awesome life this man has had! It was such a blessing to see that no matter how bad you may feel you have had it in life, God will always call you out into a better life. You aren't so bad that God can't save you and bring you into His plan for your life.

Over the years, Soke Marx has gained much in the way of wisdom and insight into everyday life, spiritual matters and even the way your body and mind will do things to you. Like his other books, this book provides so much insight into things that you will be amazed at the information contained in it that seems to be especially aimed to you! That's the heart of the matter, right there!

I praise God for leading me to meet Karl Marx and know that his legacy will live on for years to come! Suffice it to say, that this 40ish, depressed, overweight, feeling like a "has-been-before-I-got-started" pastor (in between churches at this writing), has been helped by the writings of Karl Marx and his personal encouragements. They have helped me find my way through a winding maze of pitfalls, traps and unseen treasures. No doubt his books will help you too!

Steven H. Miller

Camp Point, IL

songnsword@hotmail.com
Well, here are a few more Keichu-Do Academies, dojo's or clubs.

1. Rose Sanchez Missionary to Hungary. Zichy Kastel Petof, UT. Vajta, Hungary 7041

2. Michael Kennedy, Sandan , 8132 Cranebrook Hollow, Houston, Texas 77095.

3. Paul Hutton, 150 Gore Road, Kalama, WA 98625.

4. Thierry Gouillon, 297 Rue du Gd Cerisier, Fleuvieux Arbresle, France 69210.

5. Twain and Lon Kennedy, 5206 Hanneck Vally Lane, Katy, Texas 77450.

6. Victor Marx, 5th Dan, 316 Stallion Road, Waco, Texas 76712.

7. Rachel Yasuir, 525 Kokea St. BLD #2, Honolulu, HI 96817.

8. Russell Jones, Kickboxing Academy, Baton Rouge, LA (225)752-5885

The following are essays by Pastor Karl William Marx, Sr and friends concerning the harsh effects of anxiety and panic attacks.

Pastor Karl has personally experienced the results as a victim of anxiety and panic attacks for the past 27 years and that certainly qualifies Marx as an authority on the subject. Here he has written many of his experiences as he suffered through them. This book should help the many thousands of sufferers of this terrible dis-ease. Notice I did not say disease. Rather it is a very uncomfortable ill at ease experience (dis-Ease). Reading how doctor Marx deals with some of his attacks is helpful to other anxieties. A few close friends who are also Christian Martial Artists have added their thoughts concerning how Keichu self-defense has helped them. It is hoped that in the sharing of these thoughts, the reader will be blessed and encouraged in the reading. REMEMBER IT WILL PASS!!!

Chapter One
Anxiety The Enemy Within

By Karl William Marx Sr, Ph.D.

Anxiety, that certain emotional outburst that pollutes the blood system (at least temporary I think) causing what I call a super charge like a light bulb on a 115kw line being plugged into a 210 socket. A high load of adrenaline rushing up into the brain is very similar to a dose of the illegal drug methamphetamine, or for that matter just about any drug that causes a reaction like speed, cocaine, or high caffeine intake.

Anxiety appears to be a chemical reaction like the fright or fight syndrome. Everyone who has experienced an anxiety attack might remember how it was so difficult to set still, read, and especially be able to sleep until you walked around your house or room most of the night, and even then, exhausted you might get an hour or so sleep. I call anxiety the result of *Stinking Thinking*. For I believe that thoughts in a person's mind can cause negative reactions such as mentioned earlier. If worry can (and it does) cause ulcers, then worrying about how to pay the rent or car notes, what clothes to wear, when your next meal or pay check is coming, then trouble is bound to pop you right in the face. Now the persons who understand the TRUTH of life, because they were taught by reading the WAY of LIFE, from the Holy Bible, they would be ENLIGHTENED. Now I would say that this knowledge would open their eyes to see the LIGHT.

The Light who is Jesus Christ said, "Therefore DO NOT WORRY about tomorrow, for tomorrow will worry about its own things." Does that make sense to you? How about these words of wisdom, "Therefore I say to you, do not worry about your life, what you will eat, or what you will drink; nor about your body what you will put on. Is not life more than food and the body more than clothes?" Of course every "anxiety-ac" (I made that word up) should know that Christ said, "Which of you by worrying can add one cubit to his stature?" All that wisdom can be found in the Holy Bible in Matthew chapter six. We are also instructed, by CHRIST Himself many times NOT TO FEAR. Who was the person that said these famous words? "You have nothing to fear but fear itself"

Every "ANXIETY-AC" should know this information. Anxiety comes from many of the following feelings and emotions. I just call it STINKING THINKING ... Envy, Covetousness, Worry, Fear, Depression, Anger, Frustration, Disappointments, and too much Empathy. Needless to say many of us "anxiety-acs" can prevent most of the anxiety attacks by living the proper life style. I mean by that, IF we all rely on what the Bible teaches as God intended, we can eliminate a lot of stinking thinking and thus anxiety attacks. How can we not mess up if we don't even know what a mess up is? The WAY to wisdom is to study from a source that teaches this educational resource. Most Christians would not knowingly worship an idol. However how many of you know that Covetousness IS idol worship. Think about it. How many folks are living together outside of marriage? And they don't even care that God disapproves of their sinful life style.

Substance abuse, being hooked on anything that you put before God. Even relationships can become idols. When the habit becomes more important than the sin against their Creator it's an Idol. Smoking may not be a sin in itself; however the damage to the Temple of the Holy Spirit could be answered for at the Judgment throne of God. Any habit that controls you is sinful. Sex is a big one. I bet more people are hooked on sex than any other pleasure in existence.

A lot of folks are admittedly addicts of one substance abuse or another. However I would say that more couples are fornicating sexually than any other sin. That is just a guess mind you. If anything is more important to you than Jesus Christ then you're an Idol worshiper. Kind of like the fellow on Blue Collar Comedy TV. Except here you may be in worse peril than being a Redneck. As harsh and unpopular, even selfish as it may sound, if you have more love or need, for your parents, husband or wife, even your children than you do for Jesus Christ, sorry, but you're an Idol worshiper. Look! Don't get ticked off at me I didn't make the rules. God did, and you can take that up with him come Judgment day.

I just know that we all, especially we "anxiety-acs" should keep Jesus Christ first above all things, and I'm not preaching so shut up! HA!

Just read. Watch yourself; don't cop an attitude and start passing judgment on me. If what I say offends you about Jesus Christ, then GET OVER IT, or get used to it. I am telling the truth here to help the many fellow individuals who suffer from anxiety attacks. If what I say is displeasing to you, than I strongly suggest that you move to another Nation that hates the Unites States and Christians in particular. You will feel right at home over there. I for one WILL NOT be intimidated by any non-believers, that is their choice however I have a right to my choice also.

Anyway we that experience anxiety attacks must not allow the panic to oppress us and hurt us even more. Anxiety is enough by itself. Panic with it is OUCH! The pits. We must protect ourselves with KNOWLEDGE. For example a verse of wisdom that has definitely helped me get through some hard times are these words, "But thanks be to GOD, who gives us the VICTORY through JESUS CHRIST, Therefore, my beloved brethren, be steadfast, immovable, always abounding in the work of the Lord, KNOWING that your labor is not in vain in the Lord." It's the KNOWING, that is so important. How do we know? Why by reading from the Scriptures, the Word of God is supreme. It's the Yahoo! Yippee Kai Yea! Of ALL knowledge. Knowing the Pie-r-Square pi[r] 2 of something or another is not even close to the knowledge the Bible holds just for the taking. There is one catch however. No one can really get to the meat of the Good News unless they have accepted Christ as Lord and Savior. That is easy to do if you truly BELIEVE that Jesus Christ IS the SON of GOD and that is hard to do by intellectually thinking. It has to be a FAITH thing. Believing in the unseen.

Look I don't claim to know all the answers, I do know that no substance, human or otherwise can help anxiety suffers more than prayers and serving Almighty God. I have been there, done that and while medication prescribed by a medical doctor can relieve the situation it does not change the cause. Back in 1979 I was backsliding and living in sin with my live-in-girl friend. I found out that she was unfaithful and I went off the deep end. The disappointment at being betrayed became anger. I didn't kill anyone or even pound anybody's head. Instead I ate it up, but my pride was unchecked. I stewed over the affair and the frustration turned into depression. All this with in 24 hours.

I found her and her lover in a bar and restrained my fury. Hate can be a mighty conductor of anxiety. I suppose that is why the Bible teaches to forgive. I didn't though. At 5:00 am the next morning I woke up in a full on mega anxiety attack and since I didn't understand what was happening to me panic jumped on me like Hurricane Katrina gobbled up New Orleans in 2005. On a scale of 1 to 10 I was up to at 23 points on the anxiety machine. That was my worst ever. As time went by I was diagnosed with having a Passive Aggressive Personality. Bio-Polar and Dysthymic Impulse Control.

Chapter Two
Bushido, Where Has It Gone?

By Soke Karl Marx, Sr.

I wonder how many people really know what the word means. The American Dictionary of The English Language describes this term as the traditional code of the Japanese samurai, stressing honor, self-discipline, bravery and simple living. In this day and age, there are many Americans who attempt even so much to identify with the Samurai warrior of old. The headbands and samurai outfits (I'm guilty of that myself but never would any headbands), I always thought that looked hokey, kind of like the Karate Kid. HA! American Samurai? I don't think so, like they say in Japan, "Never Happen, boy-san". Americans, Europeans, no matter the nationality, you might dress like, talk like and even work out like the Japanese, however you will never really think like them, because they are raised up in the traditional mannerisms and personality shaping of their mindset. The Japanese Warrior of old is just that, in the past.

Even now in this time and age, the Japanese don't even think that way anymore. Most of the real Samurai, perished in the Second

World War. One does not witness the deep loyalty today as the old warriors had. Do any of you remember the story about the samurai whose master or as they were called back then, Warlord, was in conflict with another Warlord from another province? Well the story tells about the samurai's loyalty to his master. It was an act of the purest heroic, loyalty and showed the true essence of the Bushido spirit. I will call this loyal Samurai Ito. When the enemy overcame Ito's master's fortress and all were doomed to be killed, the Samurai bowed to his master and was given his last order of duty. "Save my son, and heir." With that, the brave samurai hacked and sliced his way through the enemy ranks, and fought his way to his own home. As he ran through the house, he switched his bundle that held his master's one-year-old son, picked up his own baby boy, and strapped him to his body.

Running on out the back door, and into the battle, he fought his way toward the river. The enemy samurai warlord recognized the great fighting samurai's technique and knew this warrior was his enemy's best and most loyal retainer warrior. He also knew that the child strapped

to his body was most likely to be the Prince heir of the dynasty. He could see the danger of the young prince's escaping. So, he shouted to his warriors to stop and kill the loyal samurai and the little prince. Ito was known as the best of the best swordsman, skilled in all weapons of his time. As he fought his way to the river where a boat awaited his adversaries fell two by two, sometimes three, and four. In total desperation, the enemy finally pulled back after losing some fifty warriors. As Ito reached the river's bank, a hundred arrows pierced his body, killing him and his son.

That, my friends, is what Bushido is really all about! It depicts the truth of a warrior's heart and loyalty beyond measure! Even past duty, on into a level of what might be called love. Another great example is found during the time of Kind David of Israel. One of his servant warriors was a mighty man on the battlefield. This fellow was called Adino the Eznite, because he had killed eight hundred men at one time; in other words, in a single day's battle. Wow, eats your heart out "Book of Five Rings!" One time, King David was setting around the camp surrounded by the enemy (Philistines that is), anyway, he mentioned longingly, "Oh, that someone would give me a drink of the water from the well of Bethlehem." So three of his mighty men broke through the camp of the Philistines, drew water from the well of Bethlehem, and brought it to their king.

Now that IS loyalty. They were actually the first Ninjas ever recorded in military history. I bet you didn't know that. Of course, Kind David was so blown away about their bravery, risking their lives like that, just for a drink of water that he would not drink. As bad as he wanted it, he couldn't. He said, "Far be it for me, O Lord, that I should do this! Is this not the blood of the men who went in jeopardy of their lives?" That also shows love and respect on the King's part, for his men.

Another great man of war who really showed the world a true bushido spirit was one of the three ninja like men who brought the kind the water. His name was Abishai. The story goes that he lifted his spear and fought against three hundred other warriors, killing them all. Talk about Bushido spirit! Now that's an example extraordinaire!

Any person willing to fight against all odds like these individuals, for their master, lord or king is definitely a true Samurai warrior in the truest sense of the word. However, these days that kind of warrior is rather extinct. Sadly, the so-called warriors of this day and age are more wannabes, than the selfless characteristics of humble minded, obedient servant minded warrior they should be. It appears that today's Martial Arts practitioner is more into their self-image and how much attention that can bring to them. Their self-promotion, who has the highest rank attitude, prevents many of them from actually reaching the height of perfection they might have other wise reached, had they not believed they were already at that level of proficiency. This is sort of like a person climbing a hundred foot ladder at night in a fog fill location. This climber reaches fifty feet and thinking he or she was at the top stopped. What would make them believe that?

Simple question to answer, I will leave it open to see how many of you can figure it out.

E-mail me your answer at keichudo1@aol.com. If you get it your IQ might be higher than you realize. Present indications show that there is very little real bushido in many martial art students. All too many martial art students and black belt instructors as well, are quitting their Masters and starting up styles of their own. Partly because of having a harsh, overly demanding teacher who acts like a military drill sergeant, (no insult intended) or because the rebellious spirit of anti-authorityism is so strong on their weak minds that they actually feel they know better and more than their instructor. This kind of disloyalty proves to be the downfall of American students and there instructors. Many times, I have witnessed instructors deserting their instructor, and then their students do the same thing to them.

Bushido is not just a word. Bushido is a way of life, a life style if you will. Like self-defense, bushido is not a past time, part time, some time, when you have time kind of thing. "Bushido!" The real thing is a spiritual expression of an inner heart and soul of being. An enigma, you might describe it as a living entity. Expressing bushido in words that everyone could understand is like attempting to explain the Holy Spirit. Only those who have understanding can grasp the significance of either.

Chapter Three

Single Energetic X-Chromosome Or Sex

By Soke Karl Marx, Sr.

The three little letters that in many cases CONTROL the WORLD! All to many individuals will beg, barrow, steal and KILL for this simple pleasure. Ironically, this action is only about 10% physical and 90% emotional. It's frightening how many men and women are willing to anger their Creator God, the most powerful force in the Universe and beyond. Sex is good, but NOT that good. Think about this; are 15 minutes to (in rare cases) an hour of sex, worth eternity in a sea of fire and damnation better known as HELL? You know what? Just because you don't believe in God, heaven or hell doesn't matter in the end. You don't have to believe that if you jump out of an airplane at thirty thousand feet without a parachute and land on the concrete pavement of a freeway, that you would have a certain death result either. It's not so much the fall that kills (although at that height the preventatives are high, pardon the pun); it's the sudden stop that crushes the life out of you.

Sex is among the hush words a lot of parents don't like to speak about, to or around their children. It is probably the most misunderstood word in the dictionary. It is also the most misused experience since Adam and Eve. To go one step further, sex is also the most abused experience of most likely all the sins in the World. IT would be a close race to see which is more often thought of, sex or religion. Too many people spend too much time doing it, or thinking about it. Men place entirely too much time being selfish, and narcissistic, with the I, me, my and mine attitude. Way too many men do not consider the emotional substance of the young lady they want to seduce. Girls are often more sensitive than the male egocentric, whose non-Christian attitude is "I want mine" thinking. As long as the thinking is not stinking thinking, this causes Anxiety. In my many lectures at public and private schools, I ask the male population to consider how they would react if some boy was trying to seduce their little girl when that time comes about in their lives. Or their younger sister. The usual response is they would kill the blankety, blank, bleep.

Then I explain to them that the girl they are wishing to have sex with is someone's daughter, or little sister. How would you feel Dad, and Mother as well, if you were aware that some boy was conspiring in his mind how he was going to get your 13-year-old daughter to have sex with him? Now some of you my faithful readers might be shocked about my subject of discussion. I will not apologize; I will just advise you to GET OVER IT! I am speaking truth. Outside of marriage, girls should know that most fellows that are trying to have sex with them are never worth the risk. Besides, if a guy walked up to you and called you a prostitute, or any of the other terrible names that describe that profession, you would SLAP his face. Or better still BREAK his NOSE. He might not say it to your face; however, he is thinking and hoping that you are EASY and naive. He does not really care for you, or truly love you if he's trying to have sex with you.

Sure, if you're a fine foxy sweet thing most any man will want you. That's to be expected. However, lusting for your body is a different thing. OK! So a lot of girls/women enjoying turning fellows on. You get a kick out of being swanked out and scoped by men. That is not without negative results. Either for you or some other innocent female who gets attacked by the predator YOU turned on. Showing guys almost what they want by wearing pants or anything that is just an inch or less from your pubic area and the cleavage you proudly display, is like allowing a pit bull to smell a kitty cat. That usually ends up with the cat neck deep in the dog's mouth. Come on girls, a lot of men have the mentality that if you show it you'll go it. Remember if you act like, talk like, and dress like a Call girl, you're very likely to be treated LIKE ONE. Remember ladies respect is an EARNED quality.

You want self-defense? Then don't go where the tigers live. Advice - dress appropriately - Stay out of bars and certain places where substance abuse is frequent. Nightclubs, dance halls and such. Yes I know that sounds like you can't do anything that's fun because it's a sin; however, that is not the case. If you walk in a minefield you might get blown to bits. If you swim in shark-infested waters, you might become fish food for the big white one. Fist fighting a wild Grizzly bear is stupid, and getting into the ring with the likes of an Octagon Ultimate Fighting Champion like Matt Hughes or Ice-man Chuck Liddell, is definitely a bad idea. So ladies, there you have it. Believe it or not.

Chapter Four
What is Christian Karate?

By R.L. "Duke" Tirschel

I saw a horsefly once, but I never really saw a horse fly. Words we use in connection with each other can sometimes lead our understanding down the wrong path.

One of my students from my Christian Karate Academy in Georgia can stand right next to a student of mine who attends Tirschel Karate Studio and I can't tell one from the other. One says he studies Christian Karate and the other says he studies the Chuck Norris Karate system. They both do a sidekick and I can't say, "Oh, that one on the left is a Christian sidekick and the other is just a sidekick." So then, what is "Christian" karate?

First of all, the word karate simply means empty hands, Kara (empty) Te (Hands). I'm sorry if someone, other than a Christian, documented the particular empty hand moves that they found effective in protecting their life and property. I doubt if anyone truly knows who the first man was to protect himself without the use of a weapon. It has been said that the ancient warlords did not allow monks to carry weapons. And so, if that was the case, I can see that the monks in the East, who traveled from monastery to monastery, had great cause to document what was effective for them in protecting their lives.

If they were Buddhists who did this first, then so be it. They were just Buddhists doing karate. That doesn't make anyone who does karate a Buddhist. I heard the monks were good tillers of the ground, but I would not call today's farmers Buddhists. I'm sure they cleaned their quarters and probably used a broom to sweep the floor but that doesn't stop me from using brooms. If they used karate to defend themselves, or as a sport, for whatever reason, that doesn't make me a Buddhist if I study methods of an empty handed martial art. Nor are you a Christian, just because you study karate at a school known as a Christian Karate School.

I started out saying that some words we use in connection with each other, can lead us into a wrong understanding. A Christian is a Christian, karate is karate, and a school is a school, nothing more, nothing less. On the other hand, these words used together such as in "Christian Karate School" means nothing more than a school whereby one can learn an empty handed form of martial art against the background of Christian principals. Teaching a Martial Art involves a great deal of responsibility. The physical and mental safety of a martial art student is at stake. Their impressionable minds are vulnerable to a number of ways to which they can be slanted. Instructors on both sides of that illusive line we say separate right from wrong knows this. When we limit the teaching of anything to just the physical and mental aspects there will be something left out, and that is the spiritual aspect.

In 1958, I was training in a boxing gym on a Marine Corps base, and that is where I first saw the sign "Physical-Mental-Spiritual". Since then I began to see, in many other ways that we, as human beings, are tribunal. There are three most prominent sides of our existence that need attention in order to grow to be a fully functioning person. (There are many other important areas but they can be found in these three.)

Many of us train hard to take care of the physical side and we educate ourselves about ourselves and earn our degrees on the outside, to acquire our mental capacity. But, on the spiritual level, too many of us either take it for granted, or think that the spiritual is an area over which we have no control and so neglect.

In every worthwhile pursuit in life, you will do your best if you learn to improve the physical, mental and spiritual aspects involved in your endeavor. I don't care if it is horseback riding, tennis, cooking, taking care of pets or karate. Too bring your spiritual side of your existence into play with your mental and physical doesn't make it a cult, is just makes it good judgment and common sense. No venue, no activity, nor any endeavor I know is owned by any brand of spirituality.

Oriental philosophy was prevalent in martial arts once. It was even thought to be a needed part of the training when it was first accepted in the United States. I would watch classes being held and someone who had no idea what they were doing sounded a gong. Everyone knelt and closed their eyes and there was silence. It never failed that if you watched long enough, that more than one student would eventually open one eye and sneak a look around the room and then close it and resume whatever it was he didn't know he was doing.

In time, "American Karate" came on the scene and we all resented that anytime there was a commercial or a print ad, we who were not oriental were not considered for the job. Chuck Norris made a break through with his Hai Karate cologne commercial. We did away with the meditation and the gongs and did things the American way. We got into the "softening "of the martial aspects of training with good old American Positive Mental Attitude and our creeds, "Look for the good in all people and make them feel worthwhile." I believe this was the American answer to the Oriental Philosophy that did not fit our culture.

Eventually, "Christian Karate" emerged and so schools began to open up and teach martial art concepts against a spiritual backdrop. This backdrop is the fruit of the Spirit, and is the result of the human spirit receiving the Spirit of God. Love - seeking the highest good of another person; Joy – the feeling of gladness; Peace - the quietness of heart and mind; Long-suffering - endurance, patience, slow to anger; Gentleness – not wanting to hurt someone or give them pain; Goodness - zeal for truth and righteousness expressed in acts of kindness; Faith - firm loyalty to being trustworthy and honest; Meekness - restraint coupled with strength and courage; Temperance - control over one's own passions and desires.

No organization, school, nor person is going to be perfect. Some will be right on the money and some will harm people by either going to far or not far enough. But that is exactly the reason I feel people like you are so important to society. You were so right, that the misuse of the influence given a martial arts instructor, and the quality implied to any school, because of the name they bear, should be looked at carefully. You are a pioneer in doing that, and I greatly appreciate where you're coming from. It's obvious that you care.

Therefore, you must be aware of the number of times that allegations are made of "wrong doing" by karate instructors who adhere to Christian principals. These allegations have statements that contain such words as might, can could, etc. Those words are prevalent in these recent articles questioning a karate school's use of God's word as a tool to communicate with their students. For instance, in Christian Karate: Martial Art or Cult? It says that "this thing might do that" and that could lead to this and if done improperly this over here can do these things. And then, erroneous assumptions are being made about what purposes are in the minds of all instructors who are Christian based.

Of course, I agree IF this, that and those are done for wrong reasons, there will be wrong results. But a blanket statement cannot be made about any organization or any group within an organization. That makes me wonder. I get skeptical of so much negativity about a minor portion of a large group with absolutely nothing but fear supporting the statements. "The good man brings good things out of the good stored in his heart. The evil man brings out evil things out of the evil stored up in his heart, for out of the overflow of the heart the mouth speaks."

Chapter Five
Slacking

By Karl W. Marx, Sr.

Hello again! Yes it's me all right, that old fuddy-duddy who is always getting on anyone who is slacking. If you are unaware of what a slacker is, let me educate you. A slacker is someone who seeks to avoid his/her duty. A lazy person or gold-bricker. As Christians, it is all too obvious while observing people that we know, or watching the behavior of others and ourselves can bring to light socially unacceptable behavior. It's like watching a Karate student performing a kata. If that student has not been practicing enough it shows in their technique and over all skill, or lack there of. Now don't even go there with that "I'm being judgmental," or "you're judging others" stuff. If you mess up, I'm not judging you; I'm simply OBSERVING what you're doing.

In Christian circles, people sometimes talk about certain passages from the Holy Bible, and when someone doesn't know what body of water Moses parted, so his people could cross over. It's a dead give away of their being a new believer or one who doesn't read the

Scriptures often enough. If any case, any martial art student worth his/her salt would never be caught in such a compromising position. Can you imagine a green belt student not knowing what a reverse punch is, or how to demonstrate one? Now we who are both Christian and Martial Arts practitioners have a double responsibility.

There is an image that goes with being a role model. That position cannot be tarnished by any means. Smoking cigarettes, or worse, even social drinking, hanging out in places that might stumble a young person like a local bar or nightclub, can and is, usually not a good example. Losing your temper is a large sign of mental weakness. Cursing shows intellectual language deficiency. Both of these I confess to be guilty of even today. I'm sure glad God is a forgiving creator; otherwise I would be road kill by now.

I'm also blessed because God isn't through restructuring me yet. I personally can see improvement in my behavior over the years; however it is apparent to me that I still have a long way to go. The part I must play however is NOT to be a SLACKER. Like everyone else I must focus on constantly improving. Never giving up no matter how difficult the problem becomes. I stopped drinking in 1970 when I was saved and became a Christian. I was sober for nine years and no drugs either. Am I bragging here? Nope! Just stating fact. IT CAN BE DONE! After my second marriage fell apart, I started back again but not with the same intensity as before when I was controlled by substance abuse.

From 1979 during Graduate School at North Western State University, until 1986, I existed in a living hell. Anxiety attacks took the place of amphetamines, Black Russian, Wild Turkey and various other 180 proof alcohols, plus two or three packs of cigarettes a day and that's not counting the seven times a week going out dancing to 2:00 am every night. That is NOT proper role model material. I definitely was slacking is real. I've been there, done that, and experienced the results. It HURTS like all get out. Shirking is not good. Like slacking, shirking one's duty is lazy and incorrigible.

Now for the upside, the good stuff if you will. By the power of God Almighty, and the willingness on my part to submit myself to HIS WILL, I went cold turkey, on the smoking and drinking. That was in 1986. I have been sober and smoke free every since. Praise God! "How?" you might ask. Well it was easy. The power of God is far superior during that time. Believe me the TRUTH about the wicked SHALL NOT go unpunished, to human anything. Addiction has no chance against total submission to the power of the Holy Spirit. That my friend is the answer to any and ALL addictions or bad habits. If in fact there is a difference. So get yourself Saved, Sanctified and Salvationized.

Don't be a slacker. I close with the prayer that all you reaching this will have eyes to see and ears to hear. Jesus Christ IS the WAY! The TRUTH! And the LIFE.

Chapter Six
Anxiety Attacks

By Karl W. Marx, Sr.

Well here I am again, moaning and groaning, as always, complaining about this or that, because I am painfully aware that the World around me is ruled by the evilness of humanity and definitely attempting in every way possible to be me down and ruin my walk with my Creator. After 27 stinking, horrible years of suffering from Anxiety and panic attacks, I finally learned the formula to what causes this miserable discomfort. Ouch! There for a moment I thought I was having an aneurysm. The pain in my neck was so different from others I have experienced, that for some reason the thought came to me like word of knowledge. I grabbed my Nikken Magic Wand with the two magnets and started rolling and PRAYING like all get out. That was an hour ago, the pain is gone and I'm still alive. Thank God, and my Nikken roller.

Anyway, back to the story. All these years I have been fighting anxiety attacks, and I wrote a book on how this kind of stinking thinking affects folks. However, I didn't really click until I saw a TV program kind of a Biography about on of the greatest football quarterbacks in history, namely Terry Bradshaw. He was a Louisiana boy, who rose to fame and fortune in Professional Football.

Well, according to the story, Mister Bradshaw suffered a very debilitating emotional trauma, for many years. He was a football hero in high school and college. However, when he played his first year as a pro ball quarterback, he had a bad year and a lot of that team's fans booed him and he was hurt by their rejection of him and very disturbed about what they thought of him as a play and a man in general. He was very disappointed in his ability and even more so with the attitude of the home team fans. With his later success and even a three or four time Super Bowl championships, he was still plagued with terrible anxiety attacks. As I watched the program, it turns out Bradshaw, after retiring, came to a roast or Hall of Fame even and he and his old coach

and the fans settled their differences and he is a new man. Well I don't know the exact details of his situation, but the truth came to me like a flash of lightening. BAM! You see when we stop thinking about God and start thinking about ME, things just seem to fall apart. It starts of with:

1) DISAPPOINTMENT, then comes 2) ANGER, next is 3) FRUSTRATION, after that 4) DEPRESSION, followed by 5) ANXIETY ATTACKS - physical damage.

The rest is history. As the physical body deteriorates, usually from heart complications, or mental brake down, the victim either is killing them slowly, unknowingly, or commits suicide on

purpose. People get caught up in this stinking thinking trap, because, I think, they Lion roaming around to devour us is responsible for the thinking we do. The shields we need to ward off the fiery darts (thoughts) are found in the Bible. OK! Now that you are aware of this method of self-defense, watch out. When someone or something doesn't go or turn out like you expected, and you're naturally disappointed, blow it off, and try something else. Don't sit around and mope all day. Think instead what the Bible teaches concerning that particular situation. If you don't know, then get your Bible out, dust it off and read it. There is an answer for every problem known to man, in that book. HA! Our heavenly Father had it all figured out before He even created the world and us. What do you think? God is surprised by some of the sins we commit? I don't think so. Relax! I'm not preaching to you. This is real self-defense, in the Spiritual and Mental realm. So there you have it. Complaining, griping that will not get it changed. That's why I write and expose my very heart to all who read my works. I am embarrassed a lot by confessing my failures and sins to the public and strangers. The way I see it, is that many folks don't understand me, and some think I'm a nut case. However, that's their loss! If just one individual is helped in anyway, then that's worth any disfavor I may receive from the Pharisees. HA! Jesus loves me, so there!

Most of my sorry life has been working for the other side. I am so blessed that my God is a merciful and forgiving Creator and

Savior. The Bible teaches that the wicked shall not go unpunished, and folks I can sure vouch for the truth in that. I tell you all this is not for anyone to feel sorry for me. No sir it's not sympathy I seek, understanding is the word. I want all of you reading this plain down to earth scribbling to know that no matter how much you are suffering now, God will not allow you to be

Chapter Seven
How Does It Feel?

By Karl W. Marx, Sr.

Man sometimes I think God must hate me. Of course, He certainly has a right tempted beyond what you can endure. I can assure you that sometimes and more often than I like to admit, I hurt so much that it is tempting to just give up and go back number drug, and booze I did in the past.

Only the knowledge I learned from the Bible's teachings keep me aware that what ever I suffer now is nothing compared to what Christ Jesus experienced the day of his suffering. Besides, if we just look around we will see that our plight is usually nothing compared to what others are going through. I have a severe degenerative disease of the 5th and 6th vertebra diagnosed back in 1990. Well I guess I'll keep on writing. You see, somehow I lost about 12 hours of work on this article. I wrote a little bit, then I feed my mom, wrote some more, then wash the dishes, and so on. I was on my last paragraph and shut down for the night and this morning it is gone. I was sure I had saved it several times over. But the best part of this article is lost.

I tried to find it and wasted three hours for nothing. Then I became angry and tried to delete the first part. HA! No way. I could not find the delete button on this crazy computer. So I suppose someone is telling me to continue.

Why? I don't know. However, I do know, that I probably must sound like a chronic complainer, always griping, but don't fool yourself. I am only stating facts so that others might come to know that God is always there for them. God will never allow us to be tempted above what we can endure. Others have more serious problems than we have, and we should be grateful not complaining. Please everybody, by my book, "Martial Art Spirit" then we can all discuss the different opinions, those who like it and those who don't. I wrote the book to reach the New Age Public. A lot of Christians might be offended but that's ok. We can discuss our differences. By the way, Karate for Christ is the organization along with Gospel Martial Arts Union and Gospel Martial Arts Federation; all of you should be supporting. I need the Christian view from as many as will be so brave as to buy the book and then kind enough to find the 12 non-Christian things in there. I bet you can't find them! HA! Anyway, www.keichu.com GET THE BOOK! PLEASE! HA!

Let me use myself for an example. Let's see, where do I start? OK, I'll start with Myocarditis due to Rheumatoid Arthritis. Diagnosed in 1974. Then there is the Generalized Anxiety Disorder with recurrent anxiety attacks that started in 1979 that probably saved my life. As terrible as they are panic attacks and all, God used that to strengthen my heart muscles. Somehow all those sleepless nights, walking back and forth in my apartment, was what I needed. I sure didn't like it at the time and still don't when it happens, but I am grateful to God to be alive. According to my doctor back then, I wasn't expected to live more than five years longer. It's true, he wasn't far off, I did have a mild heart attack, and a little old stroke but you see, even the medical profession can be out voted by a higher power, namely Almighty God HIMSELF. I lived in a hell like state for several years with the anxiety attacks, racking my body. In one instance I went seven days and nights without sleep and ended up in the emergency room with what I guess was another heart attack. However since my son-in-law was the one who drove me there the fellow who came in with the ambulance was taken in right away and I sat in the waiting room for three hours. Pectoral Angina was the new diagnosis in 1984 (I think) at least that was what the doctor said, according to the Veterans Clinic in Baton Rouge. There wasn't much knowledge back then concerning anxiety attacks. So the Psychiatrist I went to because I thought I was going crazy, talked to me a few minutes and incorrectly labeled me, "Manic Depressive, Bi-polar personality."

Three psychiatrists falsely labeled me with that diagnosis. Why? Because they said I was Grandiose. Yes, I told them I was a grandmaster in the martial arts and that I had schools in several places around the world. HA! It wasn't until I actually proved to them that I was who I claimed to be, that changed my rap sheet. HA! My new one was simply Dysthymic disorder with intermittent explosive impulsive control disorder. Then in 1987, I was diagnosed with having an enlarged heart due to the excessive activity; dancing every night, seven nights until 2:00 am or later in the morning. Due to anxiety walking all night long trying to exhaust myself so I would collapse into bed and sleep a couple of hours. OH! Dear God, those were some awful nights. Thank God for Christian music. I don't even want to go there with this. Know that was just the mental part of pain so inscrutably harsh that death would have been pleasant. That really hurt.

New we come to the physical pain. Are you ready for this? Check it out. In 1993 after a Lumbar MRI, this is what they reported. I had a broad-based small right lateral disc protrusion, L3-4 causing deflection of the exiting right L3 nerve root lateral to the formina. At L4-5, there was a mild circumferential disc bulge with posterior facts mildly enlarged. The combination caused moderate bilateral neuroforminal stenosis. There was slight narrowing of the central canal. At L5-S1, there was evidence of conjoined right S1 root. How does that feel? HA! IT HURTS! What in the world does all that medical mumbo-jumbo mean? It's way over my head. All I know is that the 1989 x-ray reports of my cervical spine and hands indicated cervical degeneration, of the C5-6 with neurofoaminal involvement. How does that feel? OUCH! Listen to this; I have carpal tunnel syndrome, cervical spondylosis, and C5-6 cervical radiculopathy and lumbar spinal stenosis with bilateral lumbosacral radiculopathy. For this it was felt that I might require surgical intervention. However, by the grace of God, I have been spared that experience, to date anyway. It was also felt that I was totally and permanently disabled from the above diagnostic conditions. But by the grace of God I am still here walking, (well sometimes limping) HA! But no wheelchair, thank God.

How does it feel? Pain is doable, prayer is necessary, and God is always faithful. By the way, don't you dare feel sorry for me, because al the pain keeps me praying to be relieved, blessed and able? Guess what? I am.

Chapter Eight
Talking to God

By Karl W. Marx, Sr.

Communication is a very important aspect of all God's creatures. The birds do it, the bees do it, and even the sea creatures do it. So do human beings. The problem with many humans is the lack of or the inability to communicate properly. The same can be said of many Christians. Martial Arts students are taught different techniques such as Goju-Ryu kata, Sanchin, fukyu 1, and seipai to name but a few. The instructor or Sensei, will also teach students certain stances, like kiba-dachi or zenkutsu-dachi. My point is that even American students learning a Martial Art might have to communicate in a language different from their native tongue. Talking to other individuals is crucial to many folks livelihood. A salesman, a preacher, radio announcers, all has to not only speak, but to speak properly. Talking sales to make a buck, talking trash to get a girl, talking, to hear one's self talk; people talk; about themselves, trying to impress others. So communication is vital for many of us. Oh sure, people can communicate by writing, or sign language, Morse code, or smoke signals.

When we want something we speak out and ask for it. Pass the salt please. I love you do you love me? What's up? What are you doing? It goes on and on. Yakkety yak. Communication is expressed in music, songs, poems, painting, dance and various other modes of expression. Even sports are a form of expressing something. I think we can all agree that communication at least in some degree, is a vital factor in the existence of every living creature. Who knows even atoms and neutrons might have their own means of communication. Now my purpose in writing this article is obviously to communicate to you my faithful readers. I suppose I could call this a column, and write one every week. HA! Imagine ME a columnist. With a name like I have, some folks might misunderstand and think I'm a Communist, which of course (I AM NOT).

So when we want or need something we might ask our dad if we have on living at home. Well more importantly, we all have a live in Heavenly Father, who can give us everything we NEED, not necessarily what we WANT. I want to be rich and famous; however, God in His infinite wisdom knows that if I had EVERYTHING I wanted, I might like so many others forget to pray. The children of Israel walked through the Red Sea on dry land and witnessed God's awesome power as the water parted and then fell back destroying the Egyptian Army pursuing them. With all that, even the Pillar of Fire leading them at night and smoke during the day, within three days THEY FORGOT! Can you believe that? Three days later they were complaining to Moses that he had led them into the wilderness to die of thirst. It does appear that all too many Christians only pray continuously when they are in trouble. I know speaking for myself I am certainly guilty of that. I suppose I am actually blessed by all the problems God allows me to experience, because I sure as all get out do a lot of praying. HA!

If you talked to you spouse or boy/girl friend as little as you do to your Creator God, I think they would be quite upset with you. Why do we not treat our God with the respect He so dearly deserves? I don't even understand myself. I wonder why I neglect to pray as much as I should and could. When I am not hurting from something I seem to wander off being busy with writing or doing things that occupy my time. Reading my Bible at least on chapter a day is a big help to remind me to converse with my God. Starting every morning with a good morning Abba, and a thankful prayer that I lived through the night, is also a nice way to start the day. You all should try it. Praying myself to sleep every night has been a tremendous relief from fear of going to sleep. Trusting in God's grace and mercy allows me not to fear the sleep Apnea, and my Abba Father in Heaven has healed and cured so many difficulties in my life, I wonder how much more healthy I could be had I prayed more? HA! Well enough for this issue. May God be with all of you my faithful readers, for it is you that inspire me to continue passing along the message I believe is from God our Father via the Holy Spirit.

Chapter Nine
Self-Defense Part One

By Karl W. Marx, Sr.

In Martial Art circles, I hear that word often. However, understanding the meaning of the term is a different story. Many individuals have as many definition of it as do religions have denominations. Ho does an instructor of self-defense differ from let's say, from Karate, Judo or Kung Fu instructor? While certainly all of these can be used in some way for self-defense, the fact remains that there is a difference. It is just my small minded opinion, so as not to offend any of you broad-minded folks that the formula for real and true self defense is on part physical, one part mental and one part spiritual. Teaching self-defense without all three parts is like cooking Chicken Gumbo without water, or leaving out the Roux, or the chicken itself. All THREE ingredients are necessary. Leaving even ONE out diminishes the value, and the practicality of the purpose. Protecting ones self is that purpose. Survival is the goal. You purchase insurance to protect yourself or your belongings IN CASE of a situation happening. Insurance will not stop a car accident, or damage to your home and belonging, and it sure as heck will not protect from physical illness. The up side of having insurance is that if you ever need it, you got it.

Self-defense is in fact a form of insurance. You might live a lifetime without needing to defend yourself. However, if statistics are correct, and violent crime in America has become a national crisis, and is in fact a result of mental health, health care and public safety systems being seriously challenged we ALL are in deep trouble. According to the Bureau of Justice Statistics, U.S. citizens age twelve or older experienced nearly 35 million crimes in 1997. Of those victimizations, approximately 8.6 million involved the violent crimes of rape, sexual assault, being robbed and nonsexual assault. I do not know how many children were mentally abused, or physically beaten in schoolyard fights or other humiliating offenses. Think about this going on, and ask yourself if you feel safe for yourself, your wife and CHILDREN. One violent crime every 19 seconds; one property crime every 3 seconds; one murder every 29 minutes; one forcible rape every 5 minutes; one robbery every minute; one aggravated assault every 31 seconds.

I have to tell you folks; it's time to get your heads out of the sand. We are not ostriches. We must look at self-defense from a proper intellectual view. Self-defense is NOT a PART TIME, SOME TIME, WHEN YOU HAVE TIME, thing. It is a FULL TIME, LIFE TIME occurrence.

Not that everyone must learn and then open the own school, however, on does not stop practicing something that is perfected only by repetition. I don't expect a lawyer to give up his practice to become a self-defense school owner. I do expect him or her to keep in practice at least as much as they do playing golf, or surfing. Self-defense is insurance against not just physical by mental and spiritual as well. Parents of those little loved ones that dictate to you who, what, when and were they do anything. GET A LIFE! Take control of your children. You don't like what I'm writing? That figures.

I don't care if you like me, or not. Get mad; get angry, get upset, whatever, just as long as you GET your children in a real self-defense school. Karate, Judo, Aikido and Kung Fu are all martial arts, and can be used as self-defense, but the real thing is pure ultimate fighting style workouts. There is an exception however, these folks are really tough and can TAKE a lot of punishment. My idea of real self-defense is to stay away from fights. If anyone like those fellows ever jumps you, cut-em, stab-em or shoot-em, and run like a grizzly bear was after you. But who am I to talk about them? I used to do the same thing with no referee and no time limits. Boxing for 13 years is not an easy way to learn self-defense, but thank God is sure was worth the pain and broken nose, to be able to take a punch and give a harder one back. Football teaches how to take a hit from a block or tackle, but not in the jaw. Judo teaches how to live through being thrown like a sack of potatoes. I wonder why that's an old saying? Who throws sacks of potatoes?

Anyway, did you know that fear of crime continues to imperil the social fabric of America? I found out that more Americans were concerned about violent crime and drug abuse than unemployment, pollution, the deficit or educational quality. WOW! Can you believe that? I don't see that in my area. Too many parents allow their children to tell them what they want to do. A great many children want to quit when they don't get promoted fast, but are too lazy to train at home with a few minutes practice in between classes. It has to be fun or I don't like it anymore! Commitment starts with the parents and the child learns about responsibility, integrity and loyalty from the role model they see before them. So I hope this easy reading article is short and worth your time.

Take self-defense seriously; don't over load your child with so many sport activities. Priority is safety, good self-image, esteem and courage. That comes from proper teaching of self-defense. Commit your child to at least a year. Then show them you are not a quitter nor will you allow them to be. Make them practice at home. Remember it is in the best interests of your son or daughter, self-defense is the best investment of money and time you can give you child or yourself. After a year of training your child will have better focus, eye and hand coordination, balance, courage and agility. These alone can help your child be better at whatever sport they choose to participate in later.

Chapter Ten
Self-Defense Part Two

By Karl W. Marx, Sr.

If you study self-defense for four years and learn all their techniques for the rank of Black Belt, yet you never practice, you will have only the knowledge and how to do a given technique. However, without practice your skill at applying techniques will be lacking. A black belt with just knowledge without skill is NOT a black belt. Knowledge without skill can be dangerous. It is for sure lacking wisdom.

The same can be said of some one who can pass the written test at the DMV to drive a car, yet has never been behind the wheel or actually driven a automobile or truck. This is only an example of incompetence. About the only thing worse than knowledge with skill, is not even having knowledge or skill. Let's go up a level. The mental level is vitally important in self-defense. Even if you have knowledge and skill, if you're too frightened to apply yourself to the occasion, you're road kill. The mind in training for personal protection is necessary. In a fistfight or in a tournament you must be able to concentrate, other wise you will be unable to apply your techniques. Forgetting, because of nervousness, often gives a body stage fright or a freeze up.

OK! Now we are ready for the BIG one. Spiritual attack is the most often used against all of us. Not having the knowledge to recognize a mental attack is bad enough, but not knowing how to defend against the wiles of the enemy is like fighting blind folded. Or with your eyes closed and ear plugs in your ears. The same can be said concerning spiritual attacks. If someone is not educated as to the contents of the Bible there is little hope of successful happiness and a joy filled life.

Let me use the automobile to illustrate my meaning concerning how we take care of ourselves physically, mentally and spiritually. Or I should say how we DON'T take care of our bodies known by many folks as the TEMPLE of the Holy Spirit. Our situation would be like if we purchased a brand new car. Then without reading the manual about how much air to keep in the tires, and what kind of gas to use regular or a higher octane, or even reading how much oil to put in and how often to change the oil, we might run amiss some where in the future, by not knowing when to tune the engine or rotate the tires. In other words, our maintenance would be lacking and the car might be worse for wear and tear. Taking proper care of an automobile will give it longer life and better gas mileage, not to mention less brake downs.

Our bodies are somewhat similar in up keep. The better care we give ourselves the longer life span and the healthier we are. Mentally IF we are aware that smoking, partying hopping, night clubbing, womanizing, substance abuse, over working, extreme sports that endanger the life of it's practitioners, any thing that produces too much stress, disappointment that turns into anger, which in turn produces depression and then anxiety, all in all this kind of living, often leads to death sooner than God had planned. Our freedom to choose is often to our demise. Intelligence is not always in the best interest of the beholder. Using myself as an example I was once tested in college to determine what my IQ was and to my astonishment it turned out that I scored a whopping 185. Which I'm embarrassed to say proved that stupidity could come from being a genius. My not being aware of the manual of life, I had a little physical knowledge of how to live properly however I didn't follow the instructions very closely, which resulted in my mental and physical impairment. Boy did I learn the hard way.

By my not taking time to read the instructions of how to maintain my physical, mental, and spiritual bodies, my human maintenance was lacking and believe me I am paying the price. Like and old car it cost more to keep me running than I would like to pay. My frame (spine) is bent, my tires (feet) have to be rotated or changed, (shoes) I need a tune up more than I can afford, (high blood pressure) thank God for insurance, and my motor (voice) sounds like a tractor. My battery (heart) is weak, and my transmission (nervous system) needs top grate fluid to keep from stripping my gears (joints) to name but a few examples or comparisons. You see when I don't read the manual of how to maintain MY body; I paid a large price for my negligent behavior, new I need a mechanic (medical doctor), to keep me going. So now we come to the Owners Manual. The author of that book is none other than God Himself, and that is the best you can get anywhere. If you're not a Christian, know this, Martial Arts like religion has some good ones and some bad ones. Self-defense is also a situational effective field. Many methods or styles are different, thus everyone has to choose which of the styles or religions he or she will study. There is still the attitudinal or how much do you want it processed to deal with. If you practice what you believe you will be better at it, than one who doesn't.

So whom do you love? Will you choose to study a Japanese style, or how about a Korean? Maybe you prefer a Chinese style? Then there are the different styles within the system. Shotokan, Goju-Ryu, yes I know most of them come from Okinawan background, so what? In the Korean ring, there is Tae Kwon Do and Hapkido, Tang Soo Do, and from China there is Kung Fu and the many styles within that. Choy Lee Fut, Drunken style, Crane style, and so on. Religion is similar, with Catholics, Protestants and the many styles within the Protestant believers, Baptist, Methodist, Assemblies of God and then First Baptist, Second Baptist, Four Square, Calvary Chapel, on and on.

My purpose in all this lead up is to open your eyes to see the reality of what self-defense actually is. The human being is different from an automobile; however the similarities of maintenance are not so foreign. Both are necessary for longer existence; or if you will, LIFE. Be it care or human both are better served if properly cared for. So if you chose a Martial Arts school that teaches an inferior style or has an instructor lacking in knowledge and wisdom, you may progress well, but to what avail? You may be a black belt in one martial art, and according to their requirements be considered to be great. However a student of another style might be only a green belt and have the skill and technique to defeat you.

The same might be said concerning different religions. Except in this section your mental and spiritual existence is at stake. If you practice certain karate style and lose in a tournament that is no big deal. However, if your religion is lacking and you stand to lose a lot more. Your up keep maintenance could take a terrible toll on your life. The incorrect spiritual understanding will always weaken your mental ability to overcome adversity. Strong spiritual knowledge brings forth great wisdom, and that in turn makes you a formidable opponent for ANY adversary, be it human, mental or spiritual warfare.

Chapter Eleven
Self-Defense Part Three

By Karl W. Marx, Sr.

Well here we go again, part three of the self-defense articles. I do pray that all you my faithful readers are getting some good from these words. Not of course for my good, but for yours. We were learning about the Spiritual aspects of self-defense. The advantage of spiritual defense is the fact that strong emotions, properly conducted make for a level thinking mental state of mind. Now that is even more important than having the physical strength of the World's Strongest Man, the skill and ability of a World Boxing Champion, and the greatest Karate or mixed martial arts champion that ever lived.

You know why? Well, I'll tell you. What good is all the physical self-defense, if you lose your mind to worry, unhappiness, depression, suicide, becoming an alcohol, or drug abuser? Think about that statement. Let's say you're the best street fighter in your city, or even state. Then your wife or girl friend leaves you for another man, because you mistreated her. Now had you learned how to treat people in a loving, compassionate way, then the odds against your bad behavior might have been different. HEY! Did you know that when you have a healthy respect or fear of someone like a huge giant of a man with a violent temper and the ability to do great bodily harm to any one who became his victim that is called understanding your limitations?

HA! Now listen to this, the fear of the Lord is the beginning of understanding. What do you think? Is God bigger, stronger and capable of much more damage than any man or groups of men? You bet your little pinky He is. Now once you have accomplished this understanding, your mind is open to receive Knowledge. At this point things start to grow intellectually for the person being described here. Understanding what is expected of us as living human beings. With this information, Wisdom is created, to give us the "when to" and "who to," aspects of the knowledge we process. Now our heart and soul are capable of discretion, which will in turn preserve us. From what you ask? Come on put it together!

This is where real self-defense really starts to being. This spiritual growth comes from the directional guidance learned from the almighty words of wisdom, not from the Sages or Gurus of old, or any other Eastern know-it-all. Little words of advice like IF we received God's words, and treasure, His commands within ourselves, THEN, are you ready for this? We will understand the fear of the Lord, and FIND the KNOWLEDGE of GOD; all the ideas of how to live our lives. Like this for instance, you want to be happy? The Bible teaches that "Happy is the man who FINDS wisdom, and the man who GAINS understanding" HA! I could go on and on, because self-defense starts with Understanding, Knowledge and Wisdom.

With all the above within us, there is an overwhelming prospect of our mental lives being very much to our advantage. Did you know a wise man makes a father glad, but a foolish son is the grief of his mother? Now, isn't that nice? Guess what? Having a good mind is also an advantage in getting along in the world. Check this out; here is what I learned in Proverbs. Treasures of wickedness profit nothing, bummer, but it's great to know. Stop all your wickedness. Now the good part is that by us being righteous we have a better chance of living longer. Honest, I quote, "But righteousness delivers from death." HAY! Don't believe me; read it yourself in Chapter 10, verse 1 and 2 of Proverbs. Honest!

Look you want a safe life style? Then go beyond the punch and kick, past the throw and choke, further than the wrist twist, and submission arm bar. Learn that the fear of the Lord prolongs death but the years of the wicked will be shortened. Now with that kind of information I believe you could truly be considered knowledgeable. Do you get this kind of understanding from a Playboy Magazine? Redbook? Perhaps Cosmopolitan, Popular Mechanics or watching pornography? NO WAY Jose! I don't think so, no-siree-bob, not a chance. So what are you going to do now? Study self-defense from some quack that has no knowledge of mental attacks, and most "oftenly" (just made up that word) used spiritual attacks. You folks had better give this article your undivided attention. It could make a big difference in your life style.

Chapter Twelve
What Happened To Love?

By Karl W. Marx, Sr.

Do any of you; my faithful readers remember how it felt to be in love with your first love? How about your second? Third? OK! My point is that the emotion of love is the most powerful emotion known to human beings. That's why God commands us to Love our neighbor as well as we love ourselves, and man do a lot of us love ourselves. Many of us are guilty of narcissism, prideful, egocentric, selfish, self-centered individual life styles. One has to be aware of course about the difference between real Love and Lust. Both emotions are responsible for setting off certain chemicals in our bodies that affect us not only physically but mentally as well. Anger and Hate are the next emotions that can and often do unhinge our personalities.

I will go into these in more detail after I cover yet another, just as powerful defective emotion, and that one is FEAR. This sinful emotion can freeze up a person's physical body where it cannot even move. Other disabling factors are robbing the individual victim of love, joy and happiness. The not uncommon fact that fear can control a person's personality to a degree of many mental disabilities, is really a bummer. A Black Belt in any martial art that freezes up when danger is present is absolutely useless. The knowledge and skill abilities just will NOT function. Therefore I assume we can all agree that emotions are an important aspect of our lives. God knows that, and made arrangements for us all in HIS Bible.

Remember in Philippians 4, verse 6, it teaches us to "Be anxious for nothing, but in everything BY PRAYER AND SUPPLICATION, with thanksgiving, let your request be made known to God." So fear is present, whom do you call? GOD, that's who! Also don't forget Psalm 27, verse 1. Wow! "The Lord is my light and my salvation; whom shall I fear?" These are but a few. Fear is a devise that the enemy uses to hold us in bondage. Now let's get back to the main topic of this article. LOVE! That emotion has to be the most misunderstood, misused, and abused emotion in existence. Hat is easier to detect. You can tell when someone is upset, angry, mad or whatever, with you. Love is more difficult to determine. A lot of folks love someone but are too shy to say so.

Many folks say they love someone, however in most cases, it isn't so! Over a period of time, minds change and false love begins to fade away. People don't really notice until it is too late that the fire in their romance is over. Christians, who are supposed to be different in knowledge and of one mind with Christ, are not immune from this terrible calamity. Divorce is many times the solution that they take. There are as many Christians getting divorced as non-believers. 50/50 is what most researchers are claiming.

So what are we supposed to do? Well I for one don't know all the answers; however as a Martial Arts Instructor I am expected to know how to defend myself and be able to teach others the defense against this kind of attack. Self-defense is not just about physical nature. If I want information about Martial arts one of the best resources for excellent research is the Washington Research Council on Martial Arts (WRCMA@Yahoo.com). Ask for Corey Minatani. If I want information about how to control my emotions, I look at the Christian Bible and that makes for great pertinent information concerning Mental and Spiritual self-defense. I learn what love really is supposed to be. Thus, I can defend myself against pretenders. Another great source of information is Gospel Martial Arts Foundation, (www.gmaf.org) and Gospel Martial Arts Union (www.gmau.org). Look up Christian Karate.

Emotions are strong manipulators, so if you're not a Christian you might still at least benefit from the information from the Holy Bible. It's not what you are but who you are that facilitates the good life. Christians have a difficult lift just as often as non-believers. The up side is that they use information learned from the Bible to overcome and deal with it better than non-believers, who unfortunately use the incorrect techniques. They usually find out the hard way. Just like a fist fighter, knowing certain techniques can give the weaker person an advantage despite the odds of a larger, stronger opponent. Knowing the knowledge of self-defense techniques that really work, rather than just a bunch of made up stuff is a great advantage against all odds. That is why when teaching self-defense, the idea of studying wisdom from the real Book of Knowledge, which is none other than the Holy Bible, is highly recommended.

Christian or not, you're a lot better off by studying the Teachings of the "Clean Dozen" not the "Dirty Dozen". The Sages of old have nothing on the twelve Apostles of Jesus Christ. OH! Shut up! I'm NOT PREACHING here. What are you so stinking afraid of? Just the mention of Jesus Christ and your skin starts crawling, that's a bad sign of HHS, DTB or SPA; or Hard Hearted Syndrome, Destined to Burn or Stupid People's Association. So what has all this to do with love? Go figure. God IS love! If you ain't got God, you haven't got love. The English is poor; however, the meaning is PERFECT. It all boils down to this. Jesus Christ IS the WAY, the TRUTH and the LIFE. Now you should know that the TRUTH would set you FREE! Bye now! Be blessed and

be smart!

Chapter Thirteen

Death! We All Face It, Sooner or Later

By Karl W. Marx, Sr.

Death is the single most guaranteed event in all our lives. This particular experience comes to everything human, and animal, and without warning in many cases. Death is a subject most folks would rather not think about. However, the reason I am writing about this tope is to awake the careless, not thinking individuals who unknowingly neglect this most important aspect of all our existence. I am not here to suggest that everyone should consistently think about death, only those individuals give some cadence to the fact that death is inevitable to each of us at any given time. Even after several close encounters with death myself, I am guilty of not thinking too much about it. Presently, I have my aged dear sweet little old mother living with me. She is 89 years young as of December and is she can recover from this, her second stroke (which she only had today) March 18, 2004 she may live to be 100 bless her.

Seeing my mother so close to death's door, and me realizing that I am 67 years old myself, brought me to the realization that I am a good 20 years over the heart attack or cancer danger age. Today I watched my 12-year-old dog as she muddles along, adjusting to her degenerative condition, few teeth and her tong hanging out of the side of her tiny mouth. Of course, this is characteristic of her breed. Anyway, the idea of time gone by hit me flat on the nose. I could go at any time, and the recent auto accident in which I fell asleep while driving could have been fatal for others and me. Only God could have prevented the catastrophe I had put myself in. Driving through a usually busy intersection, without crashing into someone was in fact a miracle. Death is probably one of if not the most feared result anyone faces in his or her lifetime.

Take me for example. Am I afraid to die? I'm not anxious to do that, however as for dreading death, NO WAY! What is death to me? It is falling asleep and waking up in heaven with Jesus Christ and all those who would be there years ago. Death is NOT a bad thing unless you're not a Born Again Christian. HA! That statement takes some of you back. OK, that's fine, just remember "The Truth Will Set You Free" and Jesus Christ admitted in public that HE WAS the WAY, the TRUTH and the LIFE. Man HE even confessed that HE was the LIGHT. Wow! And don't get so excited yet. Jesus also informed the writers of the Bible that WE yes you and I are the light of the World. That's awesome you and I are lights. So let's light up the people we can so that death is respected and not so dreaded. By now somebody reading all this is probably think that I'm nut case. Surprise! You're right! I have been certified by at least three shrinks that I am a Manic Depressive personality; you know one of those Bi-polar dudes. HA! I tried to shirk my responsibility to society by spending 8 weeks in a mental hospital, only to fail the insanity test and was asked to leave; so sick people could use the space.

I thought that was pretty cheesy since I had legitimate diagnoses of "Generalized Anxiety Disorder," recurrent anxiety attacks. Along with that I have Dysthymic disorder and intermittent Explosive impulse control disorder. If that isn't enough throw in Myocarditis due to Rheumatoid Arthritis. Angina Pectoris and I should have been dead since 1979. Heck with an enlarged heart, and numerous other lesser dangerous afflictions death has been buzzing around me for years. Heck we all die a little each day, so what's the fuss about? If everyone lived each day like it was their last day, I wonder how their lives would be changed. Death is actually the beginning of real life. God created us to live forever. Where we live, have or hell depends on HOW we live during this trial period. Then these temporary old tents we exist in deteriorate and a change of space arrives. After this physical death occurs we are freed from these remains and we live for ALL ETERNITY! Can any of you dear readers comprehend just exactly what that means?

Total and permanent existence, WOW! Forever and forever, always, never ending. Think about that. Jesus Christ promised us that HE would build us a home in heaven. Don't forget Jesus was a carpenter as a youth, so I'm betting our new heavenly homes will be perfect for each of us. Now if YOU do not accept the fact that Jesus Christ is your Savior and Lord, then you miss all the blessings Father God has for you, that my friend would be stupid. If were a Billionaire and I offered to build you the home of your dreams would you turn me down? Heck no! Well I offer you much more than a house here on this planet. Jesus Christ paid for it, in full just for you, a mansion in heaven.

We all will die sometime, but our soul will never die. That will be somewhere for ETERNITY, that my friend is a long time. Is yours going to be in heaven with Christ, or in hell in everlasting pain and anguish? This is a choice thing. God doesn't desire that anyone go to hell, however, we all have freedom of choice. If someone has a lot of personal problems, that is no reason to mess up their lives for a hundred or so years here in this life time. The sins people commit (and we all do sometimes) during the short time we have, are much too risky, because the price is way too high. As a youth I raised hell a lot. Praise God I didn't get killed and go there. It's February 20, 2005 and I'm 68 years old. How much longer do I have? Only God knows for sure. But I check the obits daily to see if I am in there. HA! It's true I think about death a lot more often than I did as a youth.

My wife and I are taking care of my 89 year old mother, and I see how I might be like if I live as long as her. I'm already forgetting things and showing symptoms of Alzheimer's. I call what I am experiencing "old-timers dis-ease." HA! Really though, death as we know it is the transformation from one form to another. You just better be ready to get the correct form. Wow! This might be a fine topic for discussion. You know, one of those, "well how do you know you're right?" deals. Or "Prove there is a God." Then there are the other scoffers who question the existence of Jesus Christ and the Devil. Let's discuss it. "I'll be your little chickadee," Doc Holiday said to the gunfighter, Reno.

Chapter Fourteen
The Thing About Keichu-Do

By Karl W. Marx, Sr.

Keichu-Do is a Cajun street fighting art. Coming from the Bayou and swamp land of Louisiana. This form of self-defense is rather unique in the unlike oriental martial arts, Keichu focuses on the realistic approach. While for tournament competition Keichu students use a sport division type of kicking and punching, katas developed from scratch, no copying from other styles and sparring developed from a boxing stance, not a horse or back stance. Keichu is not just another style developed by someone with a limited experience background. Keichu is an empirical scientifically developed street fighting system, designed to allow a person of small stature to defeat a larger opponent.

While Keichu is not a sport, many students use it just for that purpose in many instances. It is a fact that Keichu students, from white belt to master's level have won State, Regional and National Championships. The experience of the design master of this fighting style started at the age of nine, back in 1945. In a three against one neighborhood gang fight, the Keichu founder was victorious, even with a stab wound in his back, he won the battle. Orange, Texas was the sight and Marx won the fight. The uniqueness of Keichu is the manner in which it is administrated. Closely related to American boxing and French Savate. Keichu mixes in a little Judo, a cup of Jiu-Jitsu, a pinch of Kung Fu, a tablespoon of Karate and a gallon of streetwise Cajun fist fighting. Certain human targets are the specialty of the Cajun fist fighter.

All too many fighters are headhunters, groin grabbers and upper body kickers. Back fist, sidekicks, crescent kicks, wristlocks and arm bars are just a few of the favorite techniques a lot of martial art practitioner's use. A Keichu practitioner on the other hand, strikes in places many fighters don't even know they have places. For example many cases, we might strike and break our foe's hand. Another favorite attack spot is the other fellow's collar bone. We love punching people on their elbows. The Keichu system of self-defense is designed to break a bone on our opponent every punch. We almost always have a combination of at least three punches in succession. Sometimes breaking three bones simultaneously. This may sound rather cruel to the Christian mindset; however, stopping a dangerous situation before it becomes deadly, is a smarter choice.

Punching another person in the face fifty times only offers more damage to his cranium. On the other hand, Keichu warriors who are perfectly able to afflict such damage would rather refrain and just break a little bone, and stop the fight before serious injury occurs. This is the philosophy and difference between Keichu and other styles. Intellectually, Keichu is (besides being a great sport which by the way has one over 300 World Karate Championships) a thinking person's art. Why study Keichu? Why not? If you can defend yourself and win a confrontation in three seconds, rather than a fifteen-minute kick and scratch, five hundred-punch rumble, which would you rather do? Come on! You're able to read this right? OK! If you're smart enough to read, then you're smart enough to understand the reasoning of choosing Keichu.

Keichu is a complete self-defense art; physical, mental and spiritual. Not just in word, but in action as well. Our primary objective is to defend ourselves. Simply put, Keichu may not be as attractive as other more traditional arts; if you want beauty, and flash, then we are not for you. Now, if you want practical, no nonsense, just knock-em out techniques, that's us plain and simple, no frills. Learn tried and proven, rather than many spectacular but rarely if ever, been used in real fight stuff. Cajuns from Louisiana fight different than most folks. Cajuns use every conceivable attack in existence. Cigarette flick into the face of their assailant; spit on the stomach sucker punch; use their pants belt as a weapon; small rocks in their pocket works well also. Well the choice is yours. IT takes a year to really learn and practice is lifetime. "Knowledge is better used if skill is perfected." Now don't forget the other great saying, "Action is faster than reaction." Keep Christ Jesus FIRST in ALL YOU do. Don't forget where you read this. Now a bit more about Keichu, to acquaint everyone with our home brewed Louisiana style of self-defense.

Keichu-Do is the entire package. Keichu-Ryo is the Cajun Karate style, Keichu-Hoshin-Jitsu, is the Ju-Jitsu / Judo Grappling aspects, and Keichu-Fudoshin-Ryu, are the Weapons division. All in all though Keichu is just another kind of fighting, we don't claim to be better than any other style, just different in some ways. As the Founder of Keichu, my intention is to develop a special kind of attitude in each and every individual that studies Keichu. Self-Defense is not a part time, when you have the time, kind of past time. Defending oneself is a habit. Many things like other sports, such as soccer, basketball, baseball, football, might be more exciting to the practitioner. With so many people screaming, hollering, clapping and other encouraging sideline antics, it's easy to see why, especially children are pulled to those sports. However, even if one becomes a "Super-Star" making millions of dollars a year, what good is that, if you end up dead from substance abuse, or in prison for sexually assaulting someone?

Then there is the ever-present possibility of a child living a life of intimidation and fear of being beaten up by some bully. These experiences follow one even through adulthood. So how do you defend against those kinds of attacks? HA! You learn Keichu-Do. You might ask why Keichu-Do? Simply defined, because Keichu-Do IS a therapeutic recreation and rehabilitative process that my friend is the difference. Keichu is designed to teach total self-defense, PHYSICAL, MENTAL and SPIRITUAL. It is a possible conclusion that only Christian Martial Art Schools teach all three aspects of self-defense. Leaving out any one of these important parts it to not be fully prepared to defend oneself. If someone attempts to punch you in the nose, you can avoid the blow with a physical technique. However, if you're insulted, or your loved one is unfaithful, or any incident that is emotionally disturbing, what do you do? Go see a psychiatrist? In my professional opinion, NO! My having a BA degree in psychology, and graduate work as well is backing that up. If the Psychology Department at the University I graduated from would not have been filled, I could have received my Masters in that discipline. I took as many of the courses as possible, and spent several years working as a social caseworker and institutional counselor job.

The best anyone can do with emotional and mental disturbance is to turn to God and allow HIM to do His will. Spiritual self-defense is absolutely necessary when it comes to fighting principalities. Flesh and blood is easy compared to demon spiritual conflict. Spiritual warfare is by far, much more often and damaging. It can kill you without even touching your physical body. So if you're looking to protect your children, spouse or even yourself, you had better get it straight on the Spiritual infighting. Your Holy Bible is the source and being a born again Christian is the Force. That just means the Holy Spirit is a Power stronger than any and all other powers including demonic. I'm not preaching here, I'm just telling you the truth. I do have the credentials you know, no bragging, just fact. I have 50 years experience in the self-defense field. Along with the education, I think you readers out there might give a great deal of though about believing what I am teaching you here. If I am right, and I am it will server your best interest to learn total self-defense, whether from me or someone else, just be sure they teach all three aspects, and the only one's that do that are Christian, real Bible thumpers like myself.

Many students stop training because they overload themselves in college, holding down a job or two, more class hours than they should take, stinking excuses and more reasons for them not to attend self-defense lessons. There is nothing more important than the continuous study and practice of self-defense. (With the exception of being saved). Now I'm not talking about just Karate, Judo, or any of the many other martial art styles and systems. I am talking here about true total self-defense. I can't speak for any of the other styles, Christian or otherwise, but I know the Keichu system of fighting is as good as or better than a lot of stuff out there. In America, we don't have to import foreign countries to teach us how to defend ourselves. Look! A lot of you are thinking must be some kind of nut case, saying self-defense is more important than a college education. No! Education is very good, however what good is it if you have a Ph.D. and a seven-figure income if someone robs you or high jacks your car and stabs or beats you to death?

You could be mugged at an ATM machine or kidnapped; there are so many dangers in this sin-filled world. Self-defense is a lifetime objective. It never stops; do you discontinue your insurance just because you never have to use it? Accept it or not, self-defense is each of our duty, an obligation so to speak. That is an educational endeavor that might protect all your other education accomplishment. I pray you never have to use it however, like insurance; it's good to have if you ever do. So that's another warp from the Cajun Street Fighter. May God bless you and yours! If you're not a Christian, you might consider the best self-defense there is. Jesus Christ has already paid your fee.

Chapter Fifteen
What Does Keichu-Do Mean To Me?

By Heidi Sanchez

"Come to me, all you who labor and are heavy laden, and I will give you rest. Take my yoke upon you and learn from me, for I am gentle and lowly in heart, and you will find rest for your souls. For My yoke is easy and my burden is light." Matthew 11:28-30

What does Keichu-Do me to me? It is a ministry that has enriched my life beyond words, and most importantly, it is the ministry that God used to reach me and draw me to Him. After one year of concentrating on learning the techniques, enjoying the fellowship with my family and other students, something in my spiritual life was not quite right. God is so good though. He didn't send someone off the street, or a person I didn't trust to tell me that I needed to get right with Him. Through the gift of discernment, He told Soke that all was not well with my soul. I'm sure it wasn't easy for Soke to tell me, but he told me immediately at the end of a church service. I had to admit that there was an issue I needed to deal with. That night

I prayed the sinner's prayer with my husband, and turned over my burdens to Jesus.

Although life didn't magically become easy, I did receive the peace of knowing that my sins were forgiven and covered by the blood of Jesus. It is a comfort knowing that we are saved by

grace and not by our own worthiness, good deeds, or kind thoughts, because I know I would never be worthy on my own. I have been assured of my salvation through God's grace ever since. What an indescribable gift that God gives to us freely if we will just put away our pride and come humbly to Him. He waits so long for us to finally give up and turn to Him.

Someone who doesn't have a heart for Keichu-Do might make a point that God probably would have sent someone else to minister to me if He hadn't sent Soke or that I didn't really need Keichu-Do to help me accept Christ. (How could something that involves violence such as kicking and punching possibly be a "ministry")? I don't care about what might have happened. What I know is that Keichu-Do was the vehicle and Soke was the messenger that God used to speak to me. It's not necessary to justify the ministry or how God worked in my life. We don't need to please men; we just need to please God.

So, most importantly, to me Keichu-Do is a ministry that God uses to accomplish His will in His perfecting timing. Soke is specially gifted and ordained by God to head this unique ministry. The fruit born from this ministry is not always dramatic or impressive by this world's standard. In fact, I think that the most important fruit of Keichu-Do is the subtle and quiet comfort that Jesus gives to those who are seeking and hurting emotionally and spiritually.

If we are alive and have the gift of sight, it doesn't take a genius to notice when someone needs help. Many people seek out Soke because they need to talk. They always get the help they need because Soke is a very wonderful counselor. He knows how to listen and is patient and very kind. God enables him to be this way so that people can talk openly and really be ministered to. Soke's advice is not always what we want or expect to hear, but it is always in our best interest.

Soke is also excellent at spotting pride and exposing it. If we don't seek him out for help with pride, then he makes a point of ensuring we're aware of it. Somehow, he will mention it during the end of class talk, or he will tell a story about someone else who has the very same problem and how obnoxious it is. Whoever needs to hear it hears it and is usually convicted on the spot?

Because God is allowing Satan to have control of the world for a short time, it shouldn't surprise us when we see the result of or sinfulness all around us. Many of the families that come through our doors have serious issues to deal with. Broken apart as a result of divorce or other serious issues, it has been a blessing to me just to witness people getting counsel from Soke. They always leave his office looking much different than when they entered it. God uses the ministry to console the brokenhearted and to help them heal. This can be a gradual process, and it is very encouraging when people stay and continue to train and learn. They will be ministered to in God's mysterious ways. When a weary person is given hope and encouragement and redirected to Christ, it affirms in my heart that yes, God is using this ministry! God has sent each person who comes to learn for a special purpose. Soke often says this and it's very important for each student to know this. It reminds us that God has a purpose and a special plan for each of us, and that we need to daily tell God that we are ready to serve Him. He will show us what He expects. This is vital for the children and especially the teenagers to hear so that they can stay focused on serving God and looking forward to bright futures.

My personal experiences in learning Keichu-Do have been that God uses many people and different situations to speak to me. During every class I learn something new about our students and myself. It's amazing the way our attitudes are displayed so openly when we are on the

floor. It's clear right away who's really trying and who's just going through the motions. Or who's happy and who's troubled.

By nature I tend to be a quiet person. I mostly enjoy one on one conversations and interactions. So teaching isn't something that comes naturally or is easy to me. To get the class' attention it's necessary for me to talk very loudly because my voice isn't deep. The opportunity that Soke gives us to teach has helped me already in dealing with others in a more confident manner. It has forced me to come out of my shell and reach out to others. Shyness is actually selfishness and it's not what God expects from me.

Another reason that I believe God sent me to Soke was to help me prepare for the challenges of nursing school. I don't think that it is a coincidence that the "Black Belt Test" is on January 9th and my classes begin on Monday, January 11th. I returned to college seven years ago and began taking the science classes required to enter the nursing program. After completing the requirements, they placed all applicants in a computer lottery and I waited two more years for my number to come up. It was during this two-year wait that our boys and my sister-in-law Rose and I started learning Keichu-Do. If I had been able to get in to the nursing program when I wanted to, then I wouldn't have had the opportunity to learn Keichu-Do. But God's timing is perfect, and this fact is a comfort to me because I know that God is in control. He knew that I needed to be saved and that Soke was going to teach me valuable lessons, therefore nursing had to wait.

It's very revealing that after writing this long, I haven't felt compelled to talk about the self-defense part of Keichu-Do until now. Most people seem to think that the kicking and punching is the most important aspect of Keichu-Do. It is a tribute to God that He uses a karate ministry to save people, but that the focus is on God and not the karate.

"Blessed be the Lord, my rock, who trains my hands for war, and my fingers for battle; my rock and my fortress, my stronghold and my deliverer, my shield in whom I take refuge, who subdues the peoples under me." Psalm 144:1-2

One of the many reasons that I enjoy Keichu-Do is that it is physically rewarding. What other sport strengthens the body and teaches you to defend your life or a loved one's life in a very direct, effective way? I don't live in fear anymore. When my husband worked nights, I used to stay awake many nights, unable to sleep. Noises outside would frighten me, and I always imagined that an intruder was breaking in. I didn't know the first thing about defending one's life and I had no immediate plans to learn. Thank God that he knows what we need and how to get us there. He surely knew that our family needed this knowledge. When Daniel and David ride off on their bicycles to public schools in the morning, I feel confident that if someone tries to hurt them, they won't be victims.

In addition to the self-defense, the physical strength that we have all gained is very encouraging. And it truly is a thrill to me to be able to kick or do a kata as well as I can. There are so many aspects to the physical side of Keichu-Do. The katas are my favorite because of the complexity of the movements and the way that they flow in a pattern. But grappling has become one of my favorite parts as well. Rose is my only partner at this point, but we have learned so much and became a lot stronger in the past two years. It's also very good "sister time." We try our hardest to get the other to tap out and it's a great feeling when we remember techniques and can apply them with success! We feel that we have really accomplished something after grappling well. Now, the judo throws are not my strong point. I need to practice them as much as I practice katas. Perhaps the judo throws are to teach me humility. Sometimes I understand how the throw should work, but applying it is another story. I won't give up, but I acknowledge that my throws present many areas for improvements!

I genuinely love practicing the art of Keichu-Do. It is a privilege to be physically able to do most of the techniques. At 34, I feel stronger and healthier than I've ever been. I do thank God for health and the experience of learning Keichu-Do. As long as God enables me, I intend to continue learning, practicing and teaching others.

One of the greatest gifts that Soke gives us is the opportunity to teach others what we have been taught. It also gives us the opportunity to minister to students and parents by teaching well and showing Christ's love by our attitude. This responsibility is extremely important because what we teach our students and how well we teach them can make the difference between life and death. Also, we represent Christ as ministers of His ministry. Are we being good examples? Are we seeing through the Soke's eye and recalling what he has taught us? When I teach, I try to show patience and proper techniques, but some are reminders that we need to focus on Jesus, not ourselves. It's very easy to get caught up in the flesh and to think that we are responsible for our successes. Any success or abilities we possess are truly gifts from God and they are not ours to claim. It's called giving God the glory.

Giving God the glory was something I wasn't familiar with until I started in Keichu-Do. I used to think that I was responsible for all the good and bad things that happened in my life that I was in control of my future based on what I chose to do. I tried to do everything on my own ability, never realizing that I should have been asking God for help in every detail, especially the smallest details. This is how we grow closer to God.

Keichu-Do provides MANY opportunities to learn to trust in God. When I was called upon to perform the first kata in front of the ENTIRE class, I wanted to crawl under a rock and hide. My heart was pounding, my legs wouldn't stop shaking and I lost my balance on the final "Back L." Instead of falling on my backside, I managed to land in a back stand. I was so embarrassed that I sat down and actually cried a little. If only I knew then what I know now. When I look back on that night and recall that awful sense of fear and silly nervousness, (Soke calls it pride and he's right), it me realize how far God has carried me in just two years.

The spiritual aspect of Keichu-Do is the most important because without a strong relationship with God, the mental and physical aspects will eventually fail and you will not succeed as a minister of Keichu-Do. I see that God will use us to accomplish His will whether or not we are faithful, but I want to be faithful and be truly used in the way that God desires. When I am sinning, I have found that I am not effective as an instructor. What we perceived as small sins are not small to God. I have learned that Satan uses his demons to attack us and trip us up to make us ineffective in ministry. I have become more aware as to the source of the attacks and this awareness helps me to resist them before they get a foothold in my life.

A major part of the spiritual training happens during the special talks that Soke gives us after each class. I wish that Soke understood how special these talks are and how much I treasure them. (Hint). We receive Bible lessons and life lessons that have helped me more than I can say. I know that others are blessed as well and I often wonder if maybe it's the only positive message that some of the children have heard that day.

The often "colorful" stories that Soke shares make the talks even more memorable, along with unsolicited remarks and questions from students. By the time Soke ends with prayer, I can hardly walk, because my knees have frozen in place from sitting too long and I usually have to wipe away tears from laughing at Soke's stories. Soke's influence in my life has been great.

One of the major spiritual lessons that I have learned through involvement with Keichu-Do is that we are not to seek to please man, but only to please God. Because of the perceived violent nature of Karate, Keichu-Do is an often-misunderstood ministry in our church and also in the community. I've heard that is really isn't a ministry at all, and that it's too violent. I used to feel defensive and even angry that others didn't see the value of Keichu-Do. I wanted to twist their arms a little and explain just why they were wrong. (That's not very Christian, is it?) With time, I realized that the most I could do was to explain how the ministry works and how God used it in my life, and then to let God explain how the ministry works and how God has used it in my life, and then to let God take over with that person. Not everyone has a heart for this ministry, because God has not called them to it or they have hardened their heart to it. Either way, God is in control. It doesn't matter what people think, but it does matter what God thinks. If we are pleasing Him and serving Him by ministering to our students according to

His will, then that is all that matters. We ultimately answer only to Him. It took some time, of course, for me to fully accept that not everyone was going to be supportive, understanding, or even a little enthusiastic. But now, I feel at peace with this and can continue on learning and teaching Keichu-Do knowing that God is honored when we are obedient regardless of people's feelings or perceptions.

I was one of the seeking students that came with spiritual, mental and physical needs. I didn't fully realize how much I needed Jesus in my life. Soke ministered to me in countless ways. Through talking, teaching, and counseling, God used him to help me overcome my fears, think more clearly, and to become physically stronger and healthier. I can never repay you, Soke, but I will try to show my appreciation by learning all that I can and by passing on to others what you have taught me.

It is very exciting and rewarding to see students make real progress when perhaps they struggled for weeks or months and then suddenly something clicks and they are able to do the techniques and do them well. I truly do enjoy the interaction with the children, especially the five to ten age group. They are still very innocent and usually very eager to please their parents and any teachers who show a sincere interest in their efforts. Teaching has been a huge blessing to me.

It has taught me to have more patience, empathy, and it has helped me to improve my techniques and to be more alert to details and immediate surroundings. It's always a challenge to hold children's interest after half and hour. So that has been a learning experience as well. Soke will gently but bluntly (only Soke is gently blunt) reminds the instructors to switch gears so that the students don't die of boredom. Some days I feel torn between holding their interest and pushing them to pay attention even when they are hot, tired and perhaps bored. It builds character to persevere when the going gets tough. I want the students to be strong and willing to be uncomfortable for a while in order to learn the most that they can.

Teaching has also been a blessing because it really is a privilege to be able to share what I have learned from Soke and other students. The best teachers are those who really care and will take the extra time to show you the smallest detail and explain why it is done that way. I remember and appreciate the special instructors who would watch until I did the technique properly. I'm sure they would rather have walked away or spent time on their own material, but they waited and watched. I want to be like them.

It is amazing to me what children will teach you while you are trying to teach them. They see the world from a different perspective and they can imagine all sorts of possibilities for using certain techniques. Children also blurt out what is going on in their home life, or if they are having problems at school. Most of the time they just need to have someone listen to what is on their mind and heart. I really love this part of the ministry and am so thankful to be a part of it. God could have places us anywhere and He placed us here. So, I want to do what God expects of me and to do it well. There are so many opportunities to minister during the course of the class, and not just with students. Often parents have questions or need reassurance that their child is doing well. The number of single parent families is high. I know that they come to karate because they are comfortable there and God will give them grace to get through their trials. Practicing Keichu-Do can also be a form of therapy for those who need to get their minds off their problems.

The second way that Keichu-Do has ministered to me is mentally. When I first started taking classes, I was not confident that I could survive or even escape from an attacker. Soke stressed mental alertness as being life-saving. I learned that victims are the people walking around with their head in the clouds. He taught me to notice my surroundings and any suspicious people. It's better to avoid risky situations, of course, but if you are in a bad place it is vital to use your head and think about options. What could I use as a weapon? How many routes of escape are there if I need them? If I am attacked in here, where will I strike my opponent first? Then how will I follow up in order to disable them and escape? Also, keeping a clear mind in the face of fear can be lifesaving. I imagine possible situations and how I could escape by using the techniques I have learned instead of shrinking in fear.

It used to be that when my husband worked the night shift, I would toss and turn in bed, imagining that someone was outside and trying to break in. Then I would further terrorize myself by thinking of what would happen next, knowing that I didn't know how to defend our boys or myself. Some nights I didn't sleep but a few hours. The sun would rise and all the fears of the night seemed silly in the daylight, but then night would come again and it would all start over. I think God that I am no longer preoccupied with fear.

"For God has not given us a spirit of fear, but of power and of love and of a sound mind."

2 Timothy 1:7

Keichu-Do didn't teach me to be fearful of being attacked. Satan did a fine job of that already. What Keichu-Do has taught me is that I am able, with God's help, to be courageous and face my fears head on. I have been equipped with some excellent tools and clarity of mind

to defend others and myself if necessary. Realistically, I know that I'm not the strongest woman, that my techniques are not perfect. But practically, I feel confident that I would not shrink with fear in an attack. I would fight for my life. And if my attackers eyeballs were gouged out in the scuffle, then he wouldn't be LOOKING to attack anyone else, would he?

Another aspect of the mental training is being aware that all of the mental attacks are coming from Satan's little demons. Soke taught me this, as well. I used to believe every lie that Satan threw my way. During tournaments I would hear a little voice tell me, "What do you think you're doing? You're not good enough to stand in front of all these people and do your kata!" Then he would point out the stern black belt judges and I would feel intimidated. And if I listened and believed it then I would shake and tremble and nearly not be able to do it. The worst times were when, instead of turning to Jesus for strength and ability, I would focus on my limited abilities and myself. That is just what Satan wanted. He wants nothing more than to make us ineffective so that we won't be able to do God's work. With time and some experience I was able to recognize the attack and get my focus back on Jesus. I would still feel nervous, but I would feel Jesus enabling and strengthening me to complete the kata with His help and not on my own ability. I am sure that He sent His angels many times to hold our legs up for those sometimes wobbly side thrust kicks. It is a blessing and a relief to be able to recognize the source of these attacks now and to refuse to believe or listen.

"For who is God, but the Lord? And who is a rock, except our God? The God who has girded me with strength has opened wide my path. He has made my feet like the feet of deer, and set me secure on the heights. He trains my hands for war, so that my arms can bend a bow of bronze. You have given the shield of your salvation;" 2 Samuel 22:32-36

The mental training we receive also involves the memorization and understanding of the material. It requires time and focus to commit to memory all of the information and then to be able to recall it for tests and for teaching it. This is a great time to ask God for wisdom and understanding, because I know that I can do nothing on my own. God expects us to ask for help in every area of our lives. It can be as simple as saying, "God, please help." He is always faithful to answer us if we will just stop and think of Him instead of ourselves.

It is interesting, too, how a person's mental state affects a person's physical ability. When I'm upset or worried about something, it makes it very difficult to concentrate and perform the techniques. And it's also dangerous. So, I've learned to ask Jesus for help and peace so that I can block out the bad thoughts. He is always faithful to answer those prayers. Sometimes it takes a little while, but when His peace comes, I know it right away. That is something important to share with students because of a lot of children and adults arrive at the dojo with their minds full of their problems and the day's events or what they're going to do after class. The opening prayer is especially important because it helps us take our minds off ourselves and directs us to Jesus.

A key element in remaining in this ministry has to trust Soke's judgment and not question his decisions. I've seen people leave because they don't agree with his methods or they are easily offended. In order to survive as a Keichu-Do student, you must learn to lose your pride and submit to Soke's authority. It doesn't happen overnight and the process is very painful at times. I've observed that if Soke can determine a sensitive area in your life, then he will zero in on it in order to help you with humility. It's amusing when he's "helping" someone else with pride because it's so easy for us to see the faults of others. It's not quite as funny when you're the next in line.

I think the title of our thesis papers should really be "What Keichu-Do and Soke Mean to Me" because getting to know and love Soke has been a life changing experience for me. I have never in my entire life met anyone even remotely like Soke, and I can confidently say that I'm sure I never will again. It isn't just one or two qualities that make Soke special; it is just everything about him, because I think of Soke as my dad. I love him unconditionally and any quirks or outbursts can easily be overlooked. Besides, he is quick to apologize if he feels he did something wrong. Soke used to become angry rather quickly (I think it's called "losing one's temper"). The first time I saw this happen was when he couldn't find ANYTHING in his briefcase during one class. One person asked him for a form. Then another asked for a patch. Well, nothing was where he thought it was and he became frustrated. While holding the handle, he flung the briefcase into the air and the contents went flying everywhere. No one said anything, but everyone quickly began to pick it all up. It was at that moment that I began to realize that Soke was a special kind of person.

Soke is our Soke and Pastor too. We are so blessed to know and love him. He is a "grandmaster" and yet he is so much like a teddy bear. He is like a real bear, too, and respect for Soke comes easily. I had only known Soke for a short time when he flung his briefcase into

the air, but his short temper didn't scare me, (not that much!). But, it did make me wonder just why he was so on edge. I soon learned that he wasn't sleeping well all, couldn't breathe well, didn't feel well, has chronic back and knee pain and was waiting for God to send him his wife. She hadn't appeared yet, and he was very lonely one top of everything else. We are so thankful that God sent Kathleen to Soke because he is like a new man!

Well, as time went on, we had the opportunity to travel to tournaments with Soke. It never failed that every trip was an adventure and something always went wrong nothing but trials and tribulations. Most of the mishaps were beyond our control such as Soke's flat tire, getting lost even with great maps, Soke's medications being stolen in New Orleans, Kino's heart attack on the way back from Riverside so through all these adventures we got to know Soke and ourselves even better. The purpose of the tournaments was to spread the gospel by being lights in the dark world of traditional martial arts and eastern mysticism. I believe that God blessed us at times when He knew He would receive the glory, and He withheld blessing when our focus was on points and trophies, instead of on serving Him regardless of whether or not we were "winning".

I know in my heart the times that I wanted to win more than I wanted to serve. And pride was at the root of those times. God knows how to deal with us when pride takes over. My humbling experience came during the 1998 Nationals in Riverside. I had been extremely nervous about doing my kata well and trying to place at the top. And later in the day, Daniel, David and I were supposed to demonstrate our musical kata. I felt pressure and more pressure, but I didn't turn to God for help tried to deal with it on my own. Rose tried to calm and encourage me, reminding me to ask Jesus for help. One thing that Rose and I did before competing was to encourage each other and to sometimes threaten if necessary. We would only threaten if the other one was being a really big chicken and whining more than usual. Well, on that day I was determined to be selfish and remained focused on how nervous I felt and myself. I then managed to fall in the middle of my kata. I know that it was one of the best things that ever happened because I felt truly humbled and I didn't even feel upset. Embarrassed, yes. But not upset; because I knew that God has allowed me to fall in order to get my attention back to Him.

"These six things the Lord hates: Yes, seven are an abomination to Him: A proud look, a lying tongue, Hands that shed innocent blood, A heart that devises evil plans, Feet that are swift in running to evil, A false witness who speaks lies, And one who sows discord among brethren."

Proverbs 6:16-19.

Notice that pride is listed first. A very special quality that Soke possesses is humility. It is shocking at times to realize just how humble he is. I don't like to hear him put himself down in any way (HINT) because we all love him and appreciate him. It is distressing to see Soke upset or feeling low when he thinks that God isn't using him and wondering why. It is easy to see that God is using Soke by the fruit that he produces. The fruit might not appear to be as exotic such as kiwis or papayas; it might be more like apples and oranges. IN OTHER WORDS, Soke might not be leading hundreds to Christ, and his present students might not be winning titles or putting on demonstrations for large audiences in fact, by this world's standards it might seem to Soke and other onlookers that God isn't using him enough, but what about the hurting people who are blessed by his personal ministering to them and their families? The students who need his guidance and instruction in order to stay on the straight path in life? The little children who are encouraged by his praise and who listen eagerly as he reads to them from God's Word at the end of class? And what about his role as husband and father and his responsibilities to God to be excellent in those positions? Because of the ways that Soke has enriched our families' lives, it is very easy for me to know that Soke is serving as a minister of God.

"You did not choose me, but I chose you and appointed you that you should go and bear fruit, and that your fruit should remain, that whatever you ask the Father in My name He may give you. These things I command you, that you love one another." John 15:16-17.

The world cannot see the really valuable fruit. Only God sees that. Concerning the mental training, an important aspect is being able to swallow your pride or bite your tongue when you're not sure if you agree with Soke's decision. There have been moments of tension when I understood why some people might choose to leave this ministry. For our family, leaving has never been an option. Personally, I feel such a strong calling to be involved that I cannot imagine living without being involved in Keichu-Do. The appreciation and love for Soke would also prevent me from ever walking away. So, in our commitment to stay, we repeatedly experience God's grace and He expects us to extend that grace to others. To me, "extending grace," means to forgive wrongs without holding a grudge, and to see the good qualities in others and not notice or dwell on their faults. Again, pride will sneak up on all of us when we are not diligently reading God's word and keeping it in our hearts. Then all sorts of misunderstandings and hurt feelings will occur between Soke and students or among students themselves. I know that Satan and his demons love to create strife in a Christian ministry. If we keep this in mind, then we will be ready to rebuke him and he will flee.

"Put on the whole armor of God, that you may be able to stand against the wiles of the devil, For we do not wrestle against flesh and blood, but against principalities, against powers, against the rulers of darkness of this ages, against spiritual hosts of wickedness in the heavenly places. Therefore take up the whole armor of God, that you may be able to withstand in the evil day, and having done all, to stand. Stand therefore, having girded your waist with truth, having put on the breastplate of righteousness, and having shod your feet with the preparation of the gospel of peace; above all, taking the shield of faith with which you will be able to quench all the fiery darts of the wicked one. And take the helmet of salvation, and the sword of the spirit, which is the word of God:" Ephesians 8:10-17.

While I have grown closer to our sons, Keichu-Do has also enabled me to stop over protecting them. The first time I watched the boys spar at a tournament I thought I was going to having to heart attack. It's not easy to stand by and watch your children get hit and kicked with the potential for a serious injury. And grappling matches were especially painful for me to watch. I disliked seeing Daniel and David being choked. I wanted to jump in a pull the other guy off; but I had to be calm and sit still. It was a lesson in letting go and letting them grow up a bit and learn how to take some pain without crumbling. They don't learn this without experiencing it firsthand.

For me too, it has been very helpful to learn how to take some pain without worrying that I'm seriously hurt. I'm not exaggerating when I say that I used to be a hypochondriac and a big baby. I used to complain about stubbing my toe and every little ache and pain. Now Rose and I compare bruises and I don't mind hurting a little because it's impossible to really get stronger without some discomfort. If I'm attacked the person isn't going to be afraid to try to knock me down and hurt me. I never understood the value of being able to take a blow without collapsing until now.

Keichu-Do has also helped me tremendously with balance and coordination. During my 34 years I have fallen more than any person I know. Stairs were my downfall, but parking lots were also a favorite falling place as well. I am so pleased to say that in the last two years I have only fallen once and I was able to do a "front fall" on our front door step without hurting anything! My balance and coordination are much better too. I used to walk into doorframes and bump my elbows and hands on them. That rarely happens now and I am sure that it's because my body is stronger, and also the kicks and katas have increased my coordination.

Learning Keichu-Do together as a family has been a very positive experience, overall. It's really fun to spend time with the boys and with my sister-in-law Rose. We can practice together and help each other with techniques. I think that we're all able to encourage each other on the best days. On other days we've learned to give each other some space. I never give up home that my husband will one day come to class, too. He has supported us being in Keichu-Do and so I have to be grateful for that.

Although the boys and I have had plenty of disagreements while practicing and preparing for demonstrations, we've been able to talk them out. I've a clearer understanding now of how the boys view the world and what they really are interested in. Through Keichu-Do we have spent hundreds of hours together, and that time has been a gift that I will cherish even more as they get older. I never want to take it for granted.

Well, the time is getting close to take the "Black Belt Test." It always seemed like the goal of the very distant future. I imagined that once a person made it to black belt then they were an undefeatable expert in self-defense. They almost seemed superhuman. I understand now that it really is true that a person begins learning when they receive their black belt. It is very important to have this goal as you train, but I do realize that the black belt isn't the end of the road. It is a very deep bend in the road. Soke has explained that really none of us are worthy and what a comfort that is to hear because I feel that I will never be worthy. I will try my best, asking God for help, and His perfect will is always completed regardless of what I do. We are so blessed to have a Soke who loves us enough to encourage us to try without adding unnecessary pressure.

"I lift up my eyes to the hills from where will my help come? My help comes from the Lord, who made heaven and earth." Psalms 121:1-2.

David says:

Let me begin by saying that before Mom started Keichu-Do she wasn't nearly as fun. She didn't laugh or smile as much and she was more serious. But after a year of Keichu-Do, all that tension and apprehension seemed to melt away. What we have now is something anybody would love. That say, "A boy's best friend is his mother" is true. After working out for over 600 hours (I've done the math) at the dojo with her, both my brother and I have noticed a change in my mother's behavior. When my brother and I first started Mom was, uh "prim and proper," but now she's one mean Mama. She at first didn't want us to start because she though karate was violent. But now, when I'm grappling with another boy, trying to make him tap out, dripping with sweat and shoving his face into the mat, she cheers me on! So my advice to all boys out there who think their mom's are old school marms is bring 'em over here!

Keichu-Do has also brought my family closer together. My aunt and mom are more like sisters than sister-in-laws and my mom is more understanding. Believe me, Keichu-Do was a change for the best.

What I plan to do with my knowledge, as a "black belt" is to continue on teaching and learning as much as I possibly can. I want to learn more about teaching effectively. I need to pray for this gift so that I can be of more value to the ministry. I intend to be more attentive to what methods are successful and what holds children's interest best. I want to be like a sponge and soak up as much knowledge as possible so that I can pass it on to our students so that the ministry can continue.

In a few days my life will drastically change when nursing school begins. I will have 19.5 units of serious classes and a full time week with homework and research papers. God has been opening doors so that I can begin to train for this. I do believe that God has called me to nursing, because of the opportunities for ministering. The experiences that I have had with patients this far has been very rewarding and I have no doubt about this calling. However, I am saddened because I know that I won't be able to be at the dojo as much as I would like to be. I'm putting it in God's hands though, and trusting that He will fix the schedule according to His will. School will not last forever, and eventually I intend to be back at the dojo to help with as many classes as possible again.

The spiritual, mental and physical training that God's has blessed me with has helped me to prepare for the next two years of school. I feel strongly that I will depend on my Keichu-Do.

Training daily: All of the sit-ups have strengthened my back, making it possible for me to lift patients with less risk of injury. The pressure from test and tournaments has helped to prepare for tests and new situations in the hospital. I pray that God will help me with the stress and that I will turn to Him for all my needs. What a privilege to have the gift of knowing Keichu-Do. I take it with me wherever I go.

In closing, I would like to say that the writing of this paper has been very enlightening. It has caused me to really search my heart. God has given me new insight into this ministry, and I have an even greater appreciation for Soke and the art of Keichu-Do.

"Be still, and know that I am God!" Psalm 46:1

Chapter Sixteen
BLACK BELT ESSAY

Black Belt Candidate: Kathleen Marx
Instructor: Soke Marx
Santa Maria, CA

Esteemed Black Belt board:

Thank you for considering my application and the opportunity to express what Keichu-Do means to me. I full believe that the Holy Spirit of God gave the system of Keichu to Soke Marx. I also believe that it is a testimony to God that the system has grown and evolved into an

Evangelical tool for spreading the Gospel. Keichu-Do is sound in principal and practice, Biblically based and proven by its fruit. We serve an awesome God and in His wisdom the tools He chooses are often more complex than we can fathom. Keichu is such a tool. The Lord can use the willing Keichu heart to change and heal the mind, body and soul.

I have been a student of Soke Marx since July 6, 1997. How we met, as well as the last five years are an example of God's grace and mercy. In January of 1997, an acquaintance from work called me; he was both a martial artist and a Christian of many years. We discussed putting the boys in Karate, and he suggested looking for a Christian dojo. His comment was to be very careful in my choices, in that you had to be willing to devote yourself entirely to the style, your Sensei and the daily regimen of practice. He felt that I would be better to avoid a Sensei that might teach some of the occult aspects of Karate. Now I see the wisdom of this, definitely a reminder to us that we have a great responsibility to those that we influence.

In the course of the conversation attending church came up. (I was divorced, living in a sinful condition and hadn't set foot in a church in 15 years.) My heart rebelled and I scoffed at this good advice but out of respect for him, I listened as he explained that just because we have a "bad experience" at church, is no reason to abandon our walk. Sin is the result of human failure, not the Gospel.

Philippians 3:9 "not having my own righteousness, which is from the law, but that which is through faith in Christ, the righteousness which is from God."

This is exactly the tool that the enemy had used to stop my growth as a young Christian. It was several years later during an Inductive Bible Study when I studied the parable of the seed, that I understood how the enemy had used my previous experiences at church to discourage me from discipleship. As a more mature Christian we all have areas of stony ground in our hearts. In a broad sense God has used Keichu to break up those areas for me. I have been instructed, as a Keichu warrior to be at church twice a week, daily read my Bible, listen to the word on the radio, work in ministry, and to have an active prayer life. I am blessed. Thank you for your guidance.

My friend then went on to tell me that he had been given a vision from God for me, and those like me a vision of Jesus on His throne weeping as he held out His hands to the souls of all the aborted children. This wonderful picture of hope and love broke my heart and started the healing process, (but it would be four years before God chose to use it for His glory).

Now that I was going to church again, I started earnestly searching the Internet websites and chat rooms for information on Martial Arts. While I learned a lot about a lot of styles that I couldn't even pronounce, I found nothing on Christian Martial Arts. The REAL MARTIAL ARTISTS would laugh at my questions (in between the electrifying contests to see whose ego was bigger). The Christian chat rooms were appalled that I invaded their space with such a question after all Christian Martial Arts were an oxymoron. Just about the time I was getting completely discouraged, the Lord blessed me with Keichu.

On July 5, 1997, we were at Camelot Park in Santa Maria, celebrating Dustin's birthday, I happened to see in a local magazine an article about this guy with an unbelievable name, who had just opened a CHRISTIAN DOJO that May in Santa Maria. As I read his description of what Keichu Do meant, I thought back to what my friend had said, still the full implication of totally devoting myself did not sink in. What is totally devoting oneself? Is it going to church twice a week; or tithing 10% of your income, or working out in a Christian ministry? At first I thought so, and like the Pharisees I thought that being a good person, and doing the same stuff as other Christians was enough.

This is where Keichu is so beautiful; teaching us the "real" word, and where Soke has a gift of discernment for those who are just going through the motions. At Calvary Chapel and Keichu, we've all heard of being born again, in fact, it is a term so widely used today in Christian circles that it has become more of a title than an actual lifestyle. Jesus told us to pick up our cross daily, and this is exactly what Keichu teaches us to do. Whether it is the regular training on our techniques, the time spent in teaching, a Saturday sacrificed in cleaning the dojo, or just focusing in on our nightly Bible lesson with Soke (sometimes it is hard to sit and listen for 20 minutes when you are tired and sweaty, but the discipline and the message are well worth it).

It was so excited to see God work in my life. Since there wasn't a number listed for this "Keichu Do" as soon as I got home, I called Calvary Chapel. Not only was Soke there, but he was passing the desk at that very moment! I later found out that he rarely attended a Saturday service, he gave me directions (we were living in Grover Beach at the time) and we agreed to meet the very next day after church. What happened next has got to be some of the strangest events that have ever occurred to me.

I walked into the dojo expected to sign two kids up for a few classes, and left with three GIs, patches, handbooks and a month worth of lessons. Wow, is he a salesman or what! My head was spinning as I recalled his thick Louisiana accent as he told me that the Holy Spirit has told him that I was the one, when I asked him the one what, he told me that we were to be married.

Hebrews 11:6 "So you see it is impossible to please God without faith, any one who wants to come to him must believe that there is a God and that he rewards those who diligently seek him."

Soke's unwavering faith in God and his willingness to trust him in this (after 3 previous marriages) has been a daily testimony to us. In fact this helped the boys and I to be able to pack our bags, leave our new home and church, and move here to be Soke's wife.

Hebrews 11:8-9 "It was by faith that Abraham obeyed when God called him to leave home and go to another land that God would give to him as his inheritance. He went without knowing where he was going and even when he reached the land God had promised him, he lived there by faith."

It has been very challenging at times to be thought of as Soke's or the Pastor's wife, but Soke has set an example of humbleness for all of his students. He encourages all of us that no matter how well we do, not to get the big head. Everywhere we have traveled we seem to run into someone that he knows whether it was Ernie Ladd at A.I.M. (Soke was the first Martial Artist to be invited to this wonderful gathering of Christian athletes); Gary Purdue at the

Living Legends, Professor Wally Jay at the World Championships, or Chuck Norris in an airport in Houston. Soke is always greeted with respect and admiration for his endurance and contributions to the world of professional athletes. He sets the example for the rest of us, by giving God the glory. I think that part of what makes Keichu work so well is that while you are training your body, you are also training your attitude, while your spirit is being fed.

For the last 21 years I have been blessed with a job as a bookkeeper. Unfortunately, I also developed an attitude of rigid-ness that amounted to prove to me that it will add up. God has used Keichu to help unbend me. Both with a stiff body and a stiff mind. Just when I thought I knew my katas so well, Soke would ask me to do it from another direction. Not a problem for most people, but for me it was tantamount to panic. Then I would catch my self-arguing with him as to why (I am still learning to be submissive). I would learn a throw, only to have him modify some aspect of it (for the better) or he would just bust out dancing at the drop of a hat, making it up as he went. I have often envied the spontaneity and flexibility that he as a Grandmaster has.

Soke and our wonderful instructors have, I'm quite sure, often been frustrated with my rigid-ness and me. I apologize for being such a persistent pain, but thank you for every technique and kata that you have taken the time to explain and bunkai-ed. Thank you for letting me ask the same question three different ways.

I have gained confidence and respect for this wonderful art, because I can see that it works. It's not flashy with scarves or pretending to be a crane; but rather it teaches the most practical way to avoid a fight or to make sure in simple moves that they are going to regret this stupid thing that they are considering. Keichu Do is a Cajun Fighting Art simple and effective.

I love the opening prayer of our katas and I actually do try and think of praying for the guy that I am about to put into the hospital. I think God for the times that he has brought me to my knees because of my pride then allowed me the grace of repentance and the strength to try again.

As a child I was always afraid of people, living out in the country, it wasn't hard to isolate myself, but deep inside I was so lonely. Sitting on the fence at night looking at the stars. That hole in my was a longing for God, the one I could trust, the only one who would love me as I was. My insecurities told me that I would never be good enough.

I was always afraid of violent people, but like most angry people, I became that which I hated most. Ready to argue at the drop of a hat, or demand my rights. Keichu has shown me through proven methods that I can defend myself and that only Jesus can give us peace. Having my rights usually translates out to the right to get even. Jesus gave up his rights for us; we need to do the same.

Soke once asked me about my fighting experience, HA! Not only had I never been in a fistfight, but also in the times that violence had touched my life, I had just buckled under. Soke was used to Louisiana women who grow up wrestling alligators and regularly beat their husbands (there IS a reason for this), not some timid little California mouse.

One of the most accepted forms of domestic violence is date rape. As a victim of this hateful crime, I can say that it is perpetuated by bullies that are 99% sure of getting away with it, and the women that accept it. The sad truth is that most young women don't even fight back to any degree. Most will not even press charges. I accepted the lies of the enemy, just as many of them do, that I was just trash, who deserved no better. Keichu has shown me that Christ-esteem is what we need.

Ephesians 1:17-18 "that the Father of Glory may give you the spirit of wisdom and revelation in the knowledge of him. The eyes of understand being enlightened that you may know what is the hope of his calling, what are the riches of the glory of his inheritance in the saints."

Now I understand that I am a chosen child of the Most High, I also know that I can take a physical blow and give a pretty good one in return. I know that I may not win, but I will not flee and by the grace of God they will know what they have been in a fight.

Soke was gracious enough to teach a very angry and uncontrolled woman in the beginning himself, despite the pain he is always in. It has been a great joy to spar with Soke; you taught me

humility but never to the point of discouragement. You gave me advice, bruises, tenacity (and sore ribs!). Now every time I spar I remember that "if you don't want to get hit, BLOCK!"

I was so angry inside when I stared Karate that when I executed a punch I would pretend that I was really hitting the person (into next week). With time and the confidence that training brings, I have lost the need for the anger, but I still see the opponent. I now enjoy sparring enough that I catch myself smiling. When I teach someone who is afraid, I tell him or her about where I was when I started. Occasionally, Soke will allow the boys and I to spar, I don't really have much hope of winning, but I always learn a lot from them. Especially when they let go and stop treating me like their mom. Then, we have fun.

Because of the close proximity grappling is my least favorite aspect of Keichu, but the one that I need to learn the most. I have promised myself that this summer I will start to learn how to do ground work. Judo has been a challenge for me to remember the subtle variations of the different throws, but it is most satisfying too for someone of my size to throw a larger person (usually my favorite uki Morgan).

Weapons are my favorite part of Keichu. Not only are they realistic applications, but also I really like the variety of weapons. I think the selection of common American farm tools shows us that we can defend ourselves with anything in our immediate setting. A broom, a fireplace poker or thermos can be used as weapons just as effectively as nunchuks or your favorite sword. This last winter I expressed an interest in learning a second weapons kata. Soke blessed me by creating in just a few days Du Baton (2 sticks) a completely new kata for the Keichu Do system.

Kata is my weakest area (in my opinion). I have always avoided anything that involved people interaction, public speaking, or even crowds. Group activities are very difficult for me. I am an emotional turtle. To be the center of attention is so painful that it boarders on the physical. I pray for God to heal me of this. And he is good and faithful to give his children what they need.

2 Timothy 3:7 "For God has not given us a spirit of fear, but of power, love and self discipline."

The Lord has used Keichu several times in these last five years to show me the error of relying on myself; I need to trust in his ability to carry me through. Last year at the State championships, I lost control of my Bo, got clobbered by this Amazon (couldn't really call it sparring, more like bam, pow, crunch and it's over). And then to top it off, I forgot my kata (a purple belt kata at that) right in front of Soke. I was so embarrassed I vowed never to compete again. (There's that ugly pride coming up again.). Then a week later Soke tells me he wants me to compete in Regionals and that he has this little known kata he wants me to learn. I was honored to do Bachaledia nidan, because it meant a lot to him, if fact it meant enough that he told everyone that I was doing it.

It took me a week to learn it off of the tapes, leaving me only 2 weeks to practice. Panic began to set in, I took a weeks vacation and really concentrated. I was determined to not fail again in front of him. Practicing it sometimes 10-15 times a day. In fact, I practiced so much that I didn't spend time in prayer or the word. As the big day came, I replaced my anxiety with more practice, instead of prayer. At the last minute, I suddenly remembered to pray. The problem was that I prayed for me, not for God to be glorified in my efforts. For the first time, I walked out calm and in control (I thought) got half way through and forgot the kata that I had lived, ate and slept for weeks.

Soke:

"The problem appears to be the old ego, and pride brothers. The higher the rank, the bigger the head, the bigger the head, the smaller the brain."

Exodus 20:1-2: I am the Lord your God, who brought you out of Egypt, out of the house of bondage. You shall have no other Gods before me."

A hard lesson to learn, but it was necessary for me to learn to trust and rely on God, to worship him, not my efforts. I know that if I had done well, I would have puffed up with false pride, thinking that it was all my efforts.

One of the areas of deepest needs in my life was the need to forgive myself of the sin of abortion. I had accepted that the Lord could forgive me, but was unwilling to extend it to myself (I kept thinking that there was redemptive power in kicking myself). One of our student's moms was involved in the Healing Hearts Ministry, Binding up the broken hearted who have post abortion trauma. Julie mentioned her ministry to me several times, but it was so painful that I couldn't even begin to acknowledge that I had one, much less that I needed help. It was 25 years in the past, and I felt like I had dealt with it. It wasn't until I actually finished the course that I came to know that abortion is not only a sin of murder, but it is grievous sin against God, and from him alone must come the forgiveness and the healing.

Psalms 51:3 "For I acknowledge my transgressions, my sin is always before me. Against you, and you only have I sinned. And done this evil in your sight."

One day at church, Julie to me that the Lord spoke to her concerning me, and would I consider taking the course at the pregnancy center. It was one of the most painful things that I have ever done, to go week after week to admit my sin and seek healing with others like me. But the vision that the Lord gave me four years earlier strengthened me. After I had finished the 12-week course, the pregnancy center was approached by our church to speak along with Norma McCory (Roe vs. Wade) during a conference for sanctity of life week. As part of an outreach ministry and a Pastor's wife it heinous of crimes, but telling my children as well. Only the incredible love of my family, and the tender mercy of God, got me through. My voice shook so much that I was sure no one could even understand me, and I cried, as I looked out at all the faces I couldn't help but wonder if this would affect the dojo, or my husband's life as a Pastor. As we finished I couldn't see God's plan, I could not even see the steps!

I was just so grateful to have survived the day. But God wasn't done with us yet, we were then asked to speak the next Sunday to our church body. After it was all said and done God blessed me so much, as one person after another came up to me and told me of their abortions, their pain, and their need for forgiveness. Many that we talked to wanted to sign up for the same classes I had taken. Thus God's healing continues. It was like a flood; I received offers of prayer, requests for prayer, cards, and letters, phone calls. Hugs, kisses, and rejoicing for my victory.

2 Corinthians 1:3-4 "Praise be to God and Father of our Lord Jesus Christ, the Father of compassion and the God of all comfort, who comforts us in all our troubles, so that we can comfort those in any trouble with the comfort we ourselves have received from God."

I have struggled with the issue of "motivation." Not so much the discipline of practice, but the question of, why am I in karate? When I had been in Keichu about two years, Soke asked each of us as to our reason for being there. When he came to me, I was so embarrassed because I didn't have an answer. Graciously, he just laughed and went on to the next student. Later that week when he was out of town, I screwed up my courage and emailed him about several messages that I had heard on the subject of God's will in our lives. I am sure that we all struggle with the questions of why, and why me. Soke's answer is applicable to Karate as well as our Christian walk. Understanding doesn't mean that I understand everything in my life, but what I do understand I (should) act upon I obedience. For hard headed students like me, it really is better at some points just to accept going the move (throw, discipline, advice) at face value, then wait to see how God is going to apply this to your life. Although I have already been extremely blessed, I am excited to see how God will use Keichu in mine in the future.

As I read Keichu's mission statement and goals, I realize that training in this style is not about me, or even about Martial Arts. It's about reaching others for Christ. Our first impact of course, is the students that we teach, and the parents that are learning and absorbing as they watch. A hard hearted parent who might never listen to Christian radio in their car, will here it in our dojo, they might avoid church, but will stay and listen to Soke speak, because their child is there.

As a student I would like to say to Soke I wish you knew how much those talks mean to us. It would be possible and even by today's standards acceptable, to not open or close in prayer. I think we all gasp a little when we are called on for public prayer, and yet what a blessing it is to be able to publicly proclaim our love and thankfulness to our Lord and Savior. I have often heard Soke say that he isn't a "Preacher" and even seen him discouraged and tempted to just skip it. But Soke, please remember as it says in Galatians 6, "let us not grow weary, while doing good." Soke, you and your instructors convict us, feed us, and even sometimes beat us (Figuratively speaking). And frankly, we love it. You show your love for God and for us by continuing to be there even when you are discouraged. You are like a bloodhound in that you hone in our pride and scold us for bad conduct; then laugh to take the sting out. You have encouraged us to be brave not only at the dojo, but to go out into the world to represent Christ and Keichu. That you would entrust us with something important, encourages us to be accountable and upright.

In going to different events I have been able to witness the difference between Keichu and other martial arts. Each style seems to have its strong points, but they all seem to be designed for (as long as you are winning) to encourage the attitude that's all about you, your school, and your Sensei's points. How refreshing to be able to go and know that we have already won just by being there and representing Christ. Our focus is not the trophy but the opportunity to witness, to console, encourage and plant seeds.

When we went to A.I.M. (Athletes in Ministry) the first time, I was able to observe first hand the world of professional athletes from all over the world. Keichu Do was invited as the first Martial Arts to be represented there. It is astounding the lengths that God will go to save the lost sheep. A fair number of these athletes had been broken in both body and spirit in order to be brought to a point of acceptance of the Lord. We talked to those who had it all, wealth, position, and the prestige of being at the top, only to have lost it all. Some had been in prison as well as those who had injuries that ended their professional careers.

A professional athlete is serious about their chosen sport; the time, energy and devotion that they invest can become their passion their God. Unless God is your main reason for doing what you do, the world can consume you without you even being aware of it. We heard this testimony over and over again. We also saw evidence of God's grace and mercy. We saw lives and families that had been restored, careers redirected.

Ezra 8:22 "The hand of our God is upon all those who seek him, but his power and wrath are against all those who forsake him"

I have seen this to some degree in our own dojo, usually evidenced in myself. How humbling it has been to get caught up in the flesh and make a stupid comment. To be met with kindness and compassion and forgiveness. Thank you to all of my fellow students and to all of the instructors for your prayers and loving attitudes.

I have seen such a big change in my sons since they joined Keichu. They have grown taller and stronger both in stature and in spirit. My love and respect has grown from our experiences at the dojo. Morgan has gained strength and focus. Dustin has lost his shyness and became a dedicated teacher. Both have become Godly men who fear the Lord (and their father) and love his word. As a mother, it has been wonderful to see them take Keichu with a willing heart. To know that they will be able to defend themselves physically in a fight, and have the knowledge and strength of word to make good choices and defend their beliefs.

For most families time spent in practicing might be time away from their families, but we have been blessed in that it usually that first time of the day that we all get together. I have learned to be more flexible in my schedule and thinking, since I have often learned of our weekend plans as Soke discusses things with the class (this teaches me to be grateful to God that I did come to class instead of skipping out and going home.

A trait that Keichu is helping me to learn is submission to authority. Submission does not mean that we are inferior to authority; instead it is the admission of the need for order and structure. Submission at home, the dojo or to our government is Biblical and a test of our love for God. Since our flesh rebels against this, the Holy Spirit and the word must strengthen us. It is a fine line to be in a position of authority and not be "authoritative" in attitude.

Philippians 2:3 "Let nothing be done through selfish ambition or conceit, but in lowliness of mind let each esteem others better than himself. Let each of you look out for not only your own interests, but for the interests of others."

I think it has helped us to be more respectful at home of each other, by practicing it at the dojo. I am still learning to accept Soke's evaluation of my progress, to submit to his wisdom and authority. I haven't yet taken a promotional test that I felt I was ready for or passed one that I felt I deserved. If it weren't for Soke I would still be a white belt! I now realize that it isn't so much the physical aspect that I'm hesitant in as the responsibility of becoming and instructor. I have never aspired to teach anyone and yet that really is the whole point of become a Black Belt. I think that being a Black Belt in any style should be a very humbling experience to realize that someone has given you a helping hand up through the ranks, or we wouldn't have made it. Knowing that you are not Jackie Chan or Jet Li, but just a beginner a baby who is now ready to take their first steps toward learning to teach and serve others.

I would like to thank all of my wonderful instructors, for their patience, dedication, and skill. Your love for Keichu and your students is evident in every class. I am often amazed at the selfless giving that goes on week after week. So thank you Jeff, Heidi, Rose, David, Daniel, Travis, Heather and Dustin. You are the roll models for us all outside of our school (but family inside my heart) thank you to Victor and Eileen Marx, the Crothers family, Danny and Kristen

Gilliland. You not only encouraged me in Keichu, but also accepted me as family. And last but not least THANK YOU Soke! You have encouraged me from day one to be the woman that God wants me to be, and you have been the "stick" to prod me towards it.

"A dream is just a dream; a goal is a dream with a plan and a deadline."
Harvey Mac

Chapter Seventeen Part One
Sleepless in Santa Maria

By Karl W. Marx, Sr. Ph.D.

Well tonight I did take my medication and went to bed around 1:15am. Drat here it is 2:23 am, I slept only a little over an hour and WAM! Here I am in Anxiety again. What's with this LORD? I tried to fight it for a while however I do not want a repeat of last night so I took another pill.

DRAT! I feel like a sissy. I hate to feel so weak that when my wife is not here I am so dependent. (She and her parents are camping and fishing for a few days) Gosh! I feel so foolish. Could this be what my son Dustin was going through when he was preparing to go into the Air

Force? God help him and me if it was. What is my lesson here? My stomach is growling like a hungry Lion, what's with that? I know God has a reason for all this, I only wish HE would teach me in a less tormenting way. Even my poor dogs are wondering what the heck is going on with this crazy human. Well whatever is going on, I can always be assured that it will not last forever and that soon the anxiety will decrease and then fade away. In the meantime this is a good time to pray. No panic occurs when I fight like this. I keep telling myself God is in control; with that information in my mind it is less stressful. Pulling Scriptures from what I have studied from the Bible earlier has been a great help. Anxiety isn't so tough, compared to the power of Jesus Christ.

Chapter Seventeen Part Two
Let's Talk, or You Read

By Karl William Marx, Sr.

Dear God, talk about tense, Lord I have had some night. My sweet little wife Kathy is going through a form of Hell at work, and I am helpless to help her. My normal non-Christian secular self wants to go out to her job location and kick the you know what out of any one giving her grief. My entire purpose in life has been to protect the innocent and weak. Now I have been known to put a serious hurt on anyone who hassled any of my girlfriends and especially any of my wives. Therefore, here, I am frustrated and unable to pop a cap into the butt of anybody. As a Christian, I must admit to having a huge amount of drawbacks. No fistfights just for the heck of it, loser buys the beer. No more playing the hustle with the girls. Ho! That was the most difficult one. However with all the down sides of being a Christian the up sides were and are a Billion to one on the win-win board. Cheese! Man there is no comparison. God wins every time, and all the time. Not being able to fight back physically leaves only mentally and spiritually. Mentally? Ha! You all know what happens when frustration is un-challenged. DEPRESSION crashes the party and havoc sticks his ugly head in and guess that joins in the melee next? You got it! Mister Anxiety.

Ok! It's tomorrow already and I am still coming back to where I'm going. Good night. Let's see where was I? Oh yeah, The Hell Party! How many people are attending these kinds of pity parties? Millions, that's how many. Victims caught like fish in a net. Tonight is better less anxiety than last night. I was up every hour on the hour as usual; man I hate when that happens. Getting upset, however that only adds to the discomfort. Actually using the up time to pray for everybody, you know, even yourself IS GOOD. Prayer is the answer to most anything that needs God's attention.

Communication is the Word; pardon the pun (if I made one). Hay look! I am not playing any of you out there, you either believe me or not. Either way it is no skin off my nose. I really do wish I were a better Christian; however God is not finished with me yet. I am truly saved, that much I know, but praise Christ Jesus He has not given up on me. I mess up so much, and I'm trying hard, but I'm still a sinner. Don't go getting yourself in a frizzy, I'm not preaching here. It just happens that the words fit the description I am attempting to inform you my devoted readers with. Ha!

You know I cannot write worth a flip, but I love all of you who just cannot wait to read what I am going to write next. I LOVE YA ALL! So let us get back to reality, REPENT! Yes, that is a good beginning. Oh! By the way, the stuff I write about is things that I personally experienced either in the past or that is going on in the present. I share this with you my dear readers NOT for sympathy but so that YOU will be in a position and have the knowledge to find relief if or when it is your turn to face the enemy. That is right, I believe there is a Satan, Devil or what ever he's called. You may not agree with me but that is your problem.

Well here it is 2:27am on a Sunday, well I should say Monday now, and I'm right in the middle of a big anxiety attack. It has been a long time since I've had one this bad. My wife is away on a fishing trip with her mom and Dad; my mom is so mixed up in her mind she sits on

the toilet with the seat down and doesn't even take her pajamas off, no wonder the floor gets wet. On top of that my dog Bonnie is in worse shape as far as anxiety goes, than me, she just peed on the carpet. Dear God what a night. I get in a lot of prayer time with these, but the wear and tear on me is ragged. The hot and cold flushes are difficult but my hearing capacity is extremely high and the slightest noise makes me jump.

Dear God, I am at your mercy during this terrible time and I pray that you will allow me to go to sleep in a little while in Jesus Christ Holy name I beg of you. I feel kind of guilty for writing that prayer because if I don't get to sleep, I might stumble someone. God forbid. He never gives or allows more than I can deal with.

Bob my cousin I am writing now to you and my family the Faulks. You may never get to read this but that's ok. I am really concerned about your Salvation. You all still are Catholic and such. I am not against the Catholic Church, no way, it's just some of the things that are taught. Expressions like "The Holy Mother Church is the one Church, true Church and only Church." That is so unbiblical and untrue. The people are the Church not the building or the denomination. Bob you and Dee should know that Christ dying on the Cross paid our Salvation Bill in full. There is nothing we can or will ever do to add to that. Bob even if you don't agree with me please understand that I have been a student of the Bible for many years. Not just reading it every day, but really looking into the text and commentaries. I have learned more than most priests know. Coming to Faith and believing that accepting Christ as our Savior, and repenting by asking God the Father to forgive all our sins, and requesting that Jesus come into our lives and for the Holy Spirit to lead, guide and be with us is the Way.

Well it's after 3:00 am I will attempt to go to bed again and I pray God will have mercy on me and allow me to sleep so until later.

Well here it is later 3:45 to be exact. Talk about feeling like a fool, well I do. I went to bed and still couldn't go to sleep. My mind will not shut off sometimes unless I tale my medication. Like a diabetic I need my medication, the same as my high blood pressure medication and other necessary doctor's prescriptions. I feel like a stinking drug addict sometimes. Well with the worse anxiety attack I've had in a while I forgot to take my drugs. Wow! No wonder I have been going crazy all this time. Fortunately I believe the Lord gives us the medical advantages we have so we can get by, however not without His help entirely. Praise God I was able to go to sleep around 4:00 am.

Being without my wife is certainly uncomfortable, but this is ridiculous. Co-Dependant is not something I relish. What could I be worrying so much about? I had a nice day Keichu class was fine. I even had one student pay for a year in advance.

Dear God is my mother going through anxiety? She is so confused and gets up so many times to go to the bathroom. That I know is bothering me tonight. She can't possibly be resting enough at night. She does however sleep a lot during the day. This dry mouth can't set still long is rather bothersome. Dry nose, as well. Dear God I am so miserable. Please help me Father ... hot and cold flashes. Yuk! Relief Lord! Please.

My mind needs to stop attempting to figure everything out. Why this, why that, is not for me to consider. Even though I trust my wife the enemy is always looking for some way to attack my trust of people. Questions like "How do you know she is really fishing with her mom and dad?" Thoughts like that, even though I know were they are coming from, never the less hurt. I do know I must stop my grumbling and complaining to others about how bad I think some people of me. Stinking Thinking is what it is. Well I think I will give the bed another try. I pray that the extra medication is enough, but in the end I do realize that God IS in control.

Chapter Eighteen
Faith, The Power Within

By Pastor Karl William Marx, Sr.

Some folks describe faith as believing in something not yet seen. I ask you what is the expressing experience of believing that Jesus Christ IS the SON of GOD. Faith is the belief that Jesus Christ was born of a Virgin, and was sinless His entire life here on earth. Faith is considered the foundation of beliefs. Christians have faith in their God and Muslims have faith in theirs. Every one has some kind of faith in something, even if they don't realize it. Every night when you go to sleep you may not think about it at the time but you are actually practicing a form of faith that you will wake up in the morning. If you're in martial arts you trust your instructor enough to believe that what you are learning is good enough, and I hope, believing you will not be killed or seriously injured while training. Trust could be considered a form of faith. If you trust me as your instructor then you must have some faith in my ability to teach you the correct way.

Without the emotion or experience, this feeling however it can be explained, if in fact in can, a person will be unsteady in their thinking. People flying on an airplane are showing some form of faith by trusting that plane will not crash. In almost every action we take the risk of something injurious happening is prevalent. So by now I feel that I can assume you have a reasonable understanding of the necessity and presence of Faith in most if not all we do. Consequently we are charged with the responsibility of having the Truth and presence of right mind, for if our faith is based on incorrectness and false teaching, we are prone to mental disability in that we can easily become a victim of our own stinking thinking. That brings me to the point of serious importance. When a person says that they believe in God and that they accepted Jesus Christ into their hearts (so to speak). What does that really mean? Was their heart in the right place? Did they really mean what they professed? WHY did they actually do it?

Was it because of their faith, or because their friends were or had done it? How do we know for sure if someone is really saved? Do we in fact really need to know? I say in some instances I might like to know if a person is really a born again, Blood bought, hand raising, Bible thumper like me. My trust in them would certainly be stronger, or greater to say the least. However it is not my opinion that is so important concerning anyone's faith except my own. It is their faith that is important to them. When someone is not sure if they are truly saved, it just could be that the Holy Spirit is alarming their inner spirit that their confession of faith when they supposedly accepted Christ as their Savior might have been lacking in sincerity. Whatever the case Faith is tested quite often in our daily lives.

Weak faith, gives little hope, and no hope can be rather depressing. Which bring me to the real reason for this article.

The Infamous K.W.Marx, Anxiety Formula

1. Disappointment can bring about;
2. Hurt feelings, which usually brings on Anger;
3. Anger unforgiven definitely will bring frustration;
4. Frustration that lingers can, and does, become depression;
5. Depression unresolved is an incubator for Anxiety, and Panic Attacks;
6. Anxiety Attacks, often cause panic;
7. Panic attacks really stink.

Symptoms of anxiety are many, namely we who suffer from them because we get blinded sided by a fiery dart from the enemy are made aware of at that moment in time we are Stinking Thinking. I say we because anyone can be affected by any of the above emotions. While Medical assistance is helpful, FAITH is the real health affecter. Anxiety is a mental attack. It is also a Spiritual assault on our minds that causes confusion, despair, and agony. Many individuals when they are new in this kind of war against principalities believe that they are going to die especially if Hyperventilation accompanies the panic assault. Man oh! Man. Then is when panic has a field day on the mind of the victim. I wrote the book on Anxiety, I have been an experienced receiver of this discomfort since 1979. When I first had an anxiety attack I thought my world was coming to an end. Considering the discomfort I was experiencing, I think I thought death would be a relief.

Even having faith may not stop the anxiety from coming, however that Faith we hold that God will NOT allow us to be tempted more than we can stand, is reassuring. By tempting, I mean the temptation to just give up, and turn to something other than God for relief. We can take our medication, but no substance abuse. My mistake earlier in life was thinking I had to have someone to talk to. While that certainly helped take my mind off the anxiety, what I needed was the Grace of God and His mercy. I had to learn the hard way that my loneness and despair were like wood in a fireplace. Stinking thinking was my Waterloo. Even with faith as little as a mustarded, I had a long time no brainier fight against myself, by doing a lot of stinking thinking. It has been a tough fight over these past 26 years, but the more I study the Word of

God from the Bible, the less anxious I become because I do less stinking thinking. My FAITH in God and His redeeming grace the stronger I become. The enemy (Devil) has little or no power over me anymore. I have been faithful to God's will in my life and He has been faithful to help me.

Faith is the key word here faith in God, believing that what the Bible teaches is what has helped me the most to come through all my problems in one-way or another. I know for sure that when I gave my life over to Jesus Christ as MY Lord and Savior, my life changed. I started having HOPE. No matter how bad my situation was at the time if I turned it over to God HE always came through for me relieving my tension and stress, and also calming my soul as the Bible teaches.

Chapter Nineteen
Getting and Giving Respect

By Karl W. Marx, Sr. Ph.D.

July 8th 2005

Not too many individuals really know or even understand what the meaning of Respect is. To them it is the quotation from some tough guy, who tells everyone that you may not like me, and you may even hate me. I can accept that, but you damn well better RESPECT me or I'll rip your face off of your skull and cram it down your throat! Not very nice to say the least however it's most effective to the one being threatened. As I understand respect, it is to be a state of being regarded with honor or esteem. It's having high regard for someone or thing. I know that being respected has to do with being shown consideration or appreciation by others. I know that being respectable is somebody that merits respect and is worthy of esteem. Now how does a person get to that position? How about becoming a Hero? Yes that would do it. Rock Stars and Sport celebrities gain high praise from the public and their fans. Along with ridiculous high pay, as do Doctors and Lawyers. Rich individuals are held in high regard as well. I have no personal problems with these folks.

They earn their keep. I might be a tad disappointed that my turning a potential mass murder personality into a law abiding citizen, thus saving one of the above from being mugged or robbed and killed.

The fantastic comedian and movie star Rodney Daingerfield used to say, "I can't get any respect!" however that is not a laughing matter. Respect is an important aspect of every person's life. Men especially have a great deal of respect because of the male dominance thing. Even in the animal kingdom there has to be an Alpha male in most creatures. When a younger male animal, be it lion, deer, ram, or whatever comes in on the scene there is a fight over who is the best of the best. Horses do it, ducks do it and certainly humans do it. Just try to steal some fellow's girlfriend or wife. You might be able to sneak around and get away with it for a while, but brother if you get caught! BAM! The point is that no matter how beautiful a woman is, nothing is worth disrespecting her man, husband, brother or Daddy. Most dads I know would pound a promiscuous boyfriend into a heap of manure, and then stomp the poop out of him. Is my language to brash? Sorry! I mean no disrespect.

My purpose is to demonstrate how some people can FEEL disrespected, even if they are not. Too many individuals wear their feelings on their shoulder like a chip. They get their feelings hurt over little or nothing. Their friends (if they have any) always have to feel like they are walking on eggs for fear of saying or doing something that might offend. The victim is not the over sensitive person it's their friends or relatives. There is an old saying that one has to earn respect to get respect. There is truth in that statement however it is not complete. Many individuals have accomplished great feats, yet are not given the respect due them. Millions of people have done magnificent things, yet no one ever heard of their talent or success. The Media is guilty of neglect and much too selective coverage. Take Michael Jackson for instance. He was not in the lime light for a few years, and we didn't hear much about him for a while. However let him mess up and the media jumped on him like bees on honey, and ants on sugar. What is the media telling the public? That to really get noticed you have to do something considered terrible by somebody? Remember O.J. Michael, Dennis, and Bundy? What's with that? OK! So I'm reaching, I'll quit! Respect is something that some folks are given, and others demand it. In the military you respect the authority over you or end up in the brig/jail in military language. You may not like a person's personality, but if that person is your employer you have to respect the fact that they sign your paycheck. Respect goes even further, there is respect for your father and mother, even when you feel that they are wrong about you dating the person whom they have know is incorrigible.

Many children are so stupid when it comes to not obeying their parent's knowledge and wisdom. Daughters often fall for the tough guy on the Harley, and boys tend to fall for the girl who is promiscuous. Just remember fellows if she is giving it to you she might not have been keeping it from others before you, and might not after. Respect is when you keep yourself pure until the wedding day. Ladies, when your boyfriend wants to seduce you, he is actually thinking and telling you he has no respect for you or your family. He considers you nothing more that a women of the streets. Actually you should punch him in the nose. It is a matter of respect. If he has none for you, then you don't owe him more than a punch in the snoot.

Now let's talk about Martial Art Instructor RESPECT. When you put your life on the line every class with a black belt who by making a simple mistake in judgment could seriously injury or kill you THAT IS RESPECT. Then there are the few too many who by their own pride and egocentric selfishness believes that they are equal to their superiors. Then they believe they are superior to everyone. This is where the danger comes in for them. For they believe they are who they think they are going to be, but are not yet there, they will stop their path and never reach the objective of their destiny.

Another way of pointing out the truth is if you read seven Chapters of the Bible, and never read any more. You will lose a lot of what God has in mind for you. The blessings that are yours to get will be missed because you did not have the eyes to see or the eyes to hear. Respect MUST be given to those who deserve it. Otherwise those who do not, knowing full well the person deserving the respect, then the disrespectful person is a stinking low down scum bucket thief. WOW! Do you think I'm being to hard on such people? HA! You better get a life yourself. Repentance is what we ALL need, and some more than others. You're either for God or Against Him. If you're a middle of the road Liberal thinking individual that believes there are many ways to get into Heaven, you had better wake up and smell the coffee!

If any of you out there in Cyber-land knows me or have heard of me, you know the following to be true. My name is Karl William

Marx, Sr. I was the first United States Citizen to my knowledge, to be promoted outside of my own organization or self-promoted, or even brother-in-lawed to the rank of 10th Dan. That makes ME the senior ranking 10th Dan native born, non-oriental in America. Believe that or not I don't really care. In the early 1970's, no one was a Tenth Dan, not even Robert Trias or Ed Parker. Two men before me (I think) promoted THEMSELVES to 10th Dan but that doesn't count here. The FACT that I am the FIRST makes no difference to the media or the other Martial Art people of this age. Can you believe that? Talk about no respect. How about my being THE FIRST individual to create a system of Martial Arts, not just a style, but a entire self-defense system. Do you respect me for that? Probably not but who cares? Between Elementary and Junior High, into High school, then into the Golden Gloves, Navy boxing team and turning Pro it is said although I think it was just how many rounds I boxed that I had a record of 133 fights, losing 7 and drawing 3 times with never being stopped except one time when I was hit with an illegal blow (my opponent's elbow) crushed the bone in my nose by accident. I had 85 knockouts or TKOs. I wasn't a good boxer by any means but I could knock someone out with a left jab or a right punch.

In my years as a bouncer from the 1960s until I retired in Alexandria Louisiana in 1979, I had many opportunities to use my skill from 1945 to this day it is said by some that knew me that I had 300 fights. Well I don't know about that, however I do know for the record that I lost only one fistfight and that was to Earl Adair aboard ship in 1958. All I know is fighting. I'm not a tough guy, like the fellows who fight in the ultimate fighting, however I was doing that without a referee or cage and no prize money, 60 years ago. Eye gouging was regular, and testicles were a target area. Biting was allowed, as was pool hall, cue sticking, but 8 ball throwing was frowned upon especially when it hit a by stander. My ability as a fighter is NOT the subject of discussion however. RESPECT is. I'm a Father dad to 10 children and grandpa to 14 grandchildren. That is a reason to be respected by it's self. Not so though. I was divorced before I could raise the first four past 6 years of age. My second marriage ended when my daughter was 12 and my son only 6. My third marriage ended in less than a year, no children, thank God.

What was the cause of all these failures? Whose fault was it? Mine? My wives? It very well could be that love was not enough to hold a marriage together without respect from both parties. Respect! Is that emotion, or feeling, really so important in our daily lives? You bet your bottom dollar it is. The husband is the HEAD of the house, and his wife MUST have respect for HIM. After all SHE is the one who ALLOWS him to be in that position. Why does she do that? Because HE first treats HER with respect. In cases were the husband is a dictatorial Chauvinist pig and has no respect for his wife, she will not respect him. He may force his position and lord it over her, IF she is weak and co-dependant, however there is little joy in their lives. Respect should be a mutual situation. As I become older and less able to perform at the level that I could at 28 years of age, I saw not only a declining of my techniques but a declining show of respect from a lot of my ranking students. Lack of respect could bring anxiety. That hurts worse than a roundhouse kick to the buttocks. Anyone out there ever experienced that? I see where I failed as their teacher because I didn't teach enough of the Spiritual aspects. I took it for granted that every student knew about the Bushido Code of Ethics. Consequently many of my students have no loyalty to me whatsoever. That is a fine example of lack of respect. I admit I'm not as able as I used to be, but I'm as able as I need to be. You see it's not important whether I'm able to win a World Championship or not, but rather if I can still wipe the socks of any of my so-called Keichu masters. My work out is only 17 minutes long. I punch the heavy bag for three 5-minute rounds. I hit, kick, knee, elbow, and head butt at least 700 strikes each round. That's 2100 hits to any person I fight. I'm only good for 15 minutes with a 1 minute holding break each round. I can tie up someone for a minute. If they were really Keichu-Do warriors they would be devoted to

Jesus Christ, and thus loyal to me their Soke. I find it difficult to understand how any supposed to be real Keichu-Do warrior, could be so inconsiderate and greedy when it comes to honor. The ultimate quality of a Keichu-Do warrior is to be devoted to Christ entirely. NO Keichu warrior would be other wise in attitude or action. Disobedience and rebellion are NOT the qualities of a true Keichu warrior.

Also Christians are expected to live above the natural world. What am I supposed to do with students who have been promoted to black belt in Keichu-Do who has lost respect for me their Soke because as they grow into young adults and what they see in me is a physically disadvantaged old man? As adults many become even less respectful because then they unfortunately believe that THEY know everything and don't need anyone telling THEM what to do. I have been taught; do not be unequally yoked together with unbelievers. Now if anyone studies Keichu-Do for 4 or 5 years, then physically passes the hours of punishing techniques and all that goes with it. Then teaches for another 4 or 5 years at his or her own school, and suddenly THEY become ALL KNOWING, WISE and WISDOM beyond EVERYONE else. HA! THEY THINK! Come out from among them and be separate says the Lord! Hay! Check it out yourself, 2 Corinthians chapter six.

Keichu is not a black belt, or even a certificate. Keichu is "Devoting oneself entirely to Jesus Christ." I ask you that are supposed to be real bona fide good and true Keichu-Do warriors, WHO is your Soke? Who founded this style that you teach? Who? Karl William Marx Sr. WOW! Is this the same man that GOD, choose to give the Stewardship, and to Shepherd Keichu-Do? So why can't you do what you are supposed to do? Without even being asked. It should not ever have to be mentioned. It is YOUR DUTY. So if I want to separate myself from any of you want-to be Keichu folks get a life! Just because you have a black belt certificate in Keichu-Do does NOT mean YOU are Keichu certified. Only up to date, current membership in the Keichu-Do Cajun Self-Defense Association is considered legitimate. In Respect to ALL members of the World Kyung-Chung-Do Self-Defense Federation, and the World Keichu-Do

Instructions Federation, all lifetime memberships will be honored. On the other hand regulations and requirements MUST be adhered too. Rules are made to keep order in and chaos out. All Instructors are still required to have their students join the Keichu-Do Kai (Keichu-Do Cajun

Self-Defense Association). That action of support is a form of Respect. This association is the Retirement fund for Soke Karl William Marx Sr, as a bountiful GIFT, for over 60 year's service. It should be given generously not as a grudging obligation.

Now money is not the object of respect. It is only a means of showing respect; a measurable source of how really faithful a person is; a Sacrifice of pride and Greed. They are put asunder by the giving of these resources. The beautiful part is that it does not cost the Instructor anything. The students donate it and ask not what your Association will do for you, but rather what YOU can do for the Association. Respect it and its founder and all its members. While the Keichu-Do is a business it is also the major contributor to the Keichu-Do Outreach Ministry. But that is a story in itself. We are discussing Respect. So let's get back to the subject.

Respect usually denotes a person who is Reasonable. Respect usually brings about an attitude of Excellence. Respect is a good sign of a person who is Sympathetic. Respect produces a personality of being Prudent. Respect is a way of showing others we are Confident. Respect is being an individual who is Thoughtful. With all this written I still feel that I have not adequately explained my version of Respect. So at this time I will close and end Part One. Until Part Two God Bless you all.

Chapter Twenty
Abba Father

By Karl William Marx, Sr.
9/23/01/

Dear Abba Father,

Well here I am again, wondering how and why, what and who. You know, HOW am I going to do whatever your will is for me. WHY I am experiencing anxiety about the things I think are necessary to reach the goals set for me. I am not really sure about just WHAT it is I am supposed to do. Then there is the WHO am I supposed to be, whatever it is I'm supposed to do PERSONALLY. I would like to write a column each week that would really reach deep inside of anyone reading it; something that would bring them closer to Jesus Christ. But who am I to do anything?

Well God has shown me that HE can and does use ANYONE. Wow! Can you imagine; being a team member with the Creator of all things; Almighty God HIMSELF? I find it difficult to understand what God would have for me to do, since I was such a rotten sinner before, and still fall more than I like to admit. It's tough to hold my temper, when

I become irritated about something. My Alligator mouth sometimes overloads my mosquito behind, much more than it should. It's easier to be a sinner, than it is to be a Christian. I found that it takes a real man to overcome so many temptations that the enemy sends. Pride is the biggest culprit, with anger stemming from it.

Not many of us are really intelligent enough to actually understand what our relationship with our GOD truly is. Try to visualize that you are the son or daughter of the richest man in the World. Ok! Now think how it would be to have a Father that could heal every, and I mean every little or big health problem you had. Think about having a dad who could cure any disease imaginable; a pop, who could cure your children no matter what their condition. Wow! It just blows my mind when I even attempt to realize how blessed we ALL are who Love Jesus Christ, who has made it possible for us to have a Daddy the likes of GOD. My dad can beat your dad, stuff. Ha! No contest. The Bible teaches us that if God be with us who can be against us? There is also a teaching about The Holy Spirit of God being stronger in us than any enemy spirit in our foes. OH! Yea! We can all be killed, murdered by stupid terrorist, smashed in an accident, have cancer, or other diseases. How do we explain this kind of disaster? Only God knows for sure. However we can be assured that what others mean for evil Jesus Christ to be with in us and for the Holy Spirit to guide and lead us in all we do. God can turn to good. When hard times do come, we must not allow our pride to take control and our tempers to flare with blame at God.

Remember that Psalms Chapter 18 verse 6 where it teaches that the Lord is on my side: I will not fear. What can man do to me? If I die, in that same moment, I open my eyes to see Christ they're waiting for me. That is very comforting to those of us who have thought it over and asked God to forgive us of all our sins.

We have asked for God's intervention when we are knee deep in Anxiety. However have we learned anything from this little book? Dear ones very close to me have shared their hearts. My Darling wife has opened her very soul in the hope that someone else might be relieved from a long lasting Burden that can cause anxiety and guilt for a lifetime. I have spoken (written) from my heart; I apologize for my lack of couth and educational ability to write professionally I only ask that you open your hearts to the TRUTH who will set you free. Christ Rules Not anxiety. So in conclusion I ask you who experience Anxiety to heed what I have written. Protect yourself from Anxiety ATTACKL AND panic attacks by keeping Christ First in ALL YOU do. Find yourself a fine Full Gospel Church, set under a Holy Spirit filled Pastor who will teach you correctly, he will not to tickle your ears, but he will teach you the Truth. Do yourself a favor. Fight anxiety with the best weapons available. The Good Word from the Bible, and most of all Jesus Christ.

To Become a Christian is the answer. Like I wrote above. Believe in Jesus Christ; accept Him as your Lord and Savior. Ask God to forgive all your sins, and for Jesus Christ to come into your heart. (1) It is not so much what you say or how you say it, But that whatever you say YOU

MEAN IT. Or if you do say it, mean it.

(1). (Karl W. Marx Sr)

Chapter Twenty-one
Hard Times, What About It?

By Karl William Marx, Sr.

Ok! So what are you crying about? Me I complain a lot about how crappy my life has been and about all the bad luck and illness I have experienced. I have been divorced three times went through about 75 relationships, that all went sour. As a counselor I can't tell you how to keep a wife or girlfriend, however I can sure tell you how to lose one. Anybody can get a girl but keeping her is the real secret of being a man. When I get to feeling depressed and anxiety starts gigging me like a sore toe, I pray a lot. It works for me. When it all looks the grim reaper would be a pleasant visitor because of the pain my body is going through, and the mental anguish my brain is fighting with, life at that time appears to suck. However with a small amount of God given knowledge I remember that the World is filled with people with many more disadvantages that my puny little problems. I have a really painful left knee that comes and goes, when it comes, I hurt like all get out. Then at least I have a leg, and sometimes it doesn't hurt me for a year or so. And for that matter, the fellow who for whatever reason lost his leg is much more badly off than I am.

When I had serious tooth infection in New Orleans some years ago, and the Hospital refused to treat me because I only had a MHO and Medi-care insurance. I spent 4 hours waiting on a gurney and then found myself being transferred to the Charity Hospital across the street. I had to set there from about 6:00am until 11:00 am in pain that was so harsh that sometimes during that time I actually would have preferred death. With all my complaining and gripping, it didn't help me, not one tiny bit. I actually tried to sneak out of the Emergency room, but was caught outside by the biggest Negro Police officer I ever saw. I suppose I might have gotten away had I not forgotten to take the I-V thing sticking in my arm. Tee-Hee. What an idiot I was. Well This nice policeman walked me back into the Hospital, were I waited for the so-called Oral surgeon, who must have received his license to practice medicine from K-Mart. Sheesh! He liked to have killed me. I was told that the seriousness of my condition that they wanted me to stay overnight.

HA! Are you kidding? They left to see other patients, and I sat there feeling sorry for myself, and gripping about my circumstances. Outside in the hall a fellow was complaining about the service there he wasn't receiving. He had been outside my room for about an hour or more himself. It seems that he was suffering from a bullet he received at the Prison riot he had been in. Can you imagine how selfish and embarrassed I felt? After all my gripping when all I had was an infected Wisdom tooth and this fellow was lying out there with a gun shot wound. I wonder how many of us that complain about "poor me" Dear God when I realize how many bad times I have suffered through, yet in just about every, if not all of these situations, someone else was worse off than me. So how can any of us complain about our losses? Someone loses a child in death, what's with the "How could GOD allow something like this to happen to *ME*, or my family? However if you stop and think, *what if* you would have lost your wife and three children because of some drunk driver?" The man who complains about losing an eye in a freak accident at work, might consider thanking God, he didn't lose both eyes.

In every case of hard times that I experienced, there was always the fact that *it could have been worse.* Folks, everything that you have been through concerning *HARD TIMES* could have been worse than what you actually experienced. Being grateful is not a bad thing. I'm not preaching here, but having God on your side is like being lost in the woods and the best guide in the World finding you. If you think you have problems, why not have the very best problem solver ever, as your friend. If someone jumps me in a Park or any were for that matter. I want Chuck "the Iceman" Liddell as my bodyguard. Dear God it is one thing to have hard times, but another in dealing with these difficult times. Having someone that we can depend on in every case is really a grand thing. It's getting through the hard times that teach us how to appreciate the good times. Having God there is always a relief and very comforting to a big sissy like me. I can get set off with a stinking anxiety attack for hardly any reason at all.

It takes just a thought, a time memory, or a possible future event that I think about, and BOY! Do I get it? The best thing about getting upset, for any reason, is the fact that not even Anxiety can defeat any of us.   Putting on the whole Armor of God and pray for every member of your family, friends, and even your enemies, HA! That one really ticks off the Devil. Grab your Bible and walk all through out your home. Demons can't stand that, "I resist you Satan" and they all have to flee.   Don't go about shouting how little old you are binding the devil, because then you trap him in your house. NO, kick him out by the power of the Holy Spirit and the Blood of Jesus. If you go to war with those fellows on your own accord, your going to get you head stomped on. Today as I write is Christmas, and this is like Hunting in a game reserve with your pray tied to a stake. The Devil has no sportsmanship ideas. He will gun you down even while you sleep. Christmas is soul and minds season.   So is New Years night. Man what a bad time to be alone.

Hard times are as regular as rain we all have them. The degree of misfortune, pain, and depression depends on our personalities. By that I mean, if we are prayer warriors, when the hard time hit us we fight with prayer, and supplication. Others fight by using alcohol and drug abuse. Still there are those who attempt to find relief by being promiscuous and fornicating like rabbits. That only adds to their misery. I found that writing my experiences as they happen helps me and while being fresh in my mind because I'm usually writing while in or just after whatever occasion or situation I happen to be in at that moment, it's fresh in my mind, accurate, and sometimes even helpful to others who may be going through or who have been through the same or similar experiences. As the chief Shepard of our LORD'S flock of sheep, it is my duty to teach, train, and prepare God's Children in HIS Ways, Commands, and Commandments.

Christ ordered Peter and the others to feed his sheep three times in the same conservation. That was NOT a suggestion.

Keichu-Do Black Belts are Missionaries in a way. Were ever God sends us and what ever employment he grants us, be it Dish Washer or Rocket scientist, Doctor or Lawyer, it is our duty to serve God by teaching HIS Word. Most of our problem is the fact we forget that our conduct ourselves by being like minded having the same love, being of one accord of one mind. Hay! The true spirit of a Keichu warrior is let nothing be done through selfish ambition, which is where I failed and so did most all of my so-called students. I didn't think of myself as conceited or prideful but I didn't fell lowness of my mind, and like so many other black belts I didn't esteem others better than myself. If anything I felt cheated because others were getting the glory that I felt should have been mine. Also, those who deserved these honors were deserved however I felt I had earned the right to be up there with them.

I forgot my purpose and lost sight of my vision. All I wanted was a great reputation and tons of respect. I could note understand why Bruce Lee was getting all the Ho-How because he was oriental and a movie star. I was doing things that he did before he did them, and I was an intelligent as him, but he was the best thing singe Jesus Christ to American martial Artist. I was so jealous I wanted to throw up every time I saw him on the front cover of so many magazines. I was a failure myself so how could I teach Keichu-Do? A failure in that while proving that my Sheep (style) was as good as or better than many of the existing traditional styles, I didn't push on the more import and aspects as I should have; that of course being the mental and most importantly the Spiritual area. With my mind on the honors from my so-called many accomplishments, our like mildness was about fame and fortune, and NOT on the Hospital of Jesus Christ.

So you see my foundation and roots were built on a sandy ground and now after all these years my house of Keichu has fallen apart. The up side of all this is that now I have seen the light so to speak, and now I can rebuild on a solid foundation using God's Word as my concrete slab. One of the first things I must do, and that is forgetting those things, which are behind and reach forward to those things, which are ahead. Now that is the way a Christian warrior is supposed to think. Hard Times have a difficult time growing on someone with that mentality. It is the Philosophy of Jesus Christ that gives power to the Christian fighter. Man when things look the bleakest and I 'm in deep depression I remember the words of Holy Scripture that teach about my needs. From following Christian Belief's I have learned that in whatever state I am, to be content. It may not be what Lao-tse might teach, in the Taoist philosophy. Or perhaps some martial art practitioners study the Philosophy of Buddhism or Hinduism. Every one has their choice, me I choose to study the Christian Philosophy. It is a strange that Martial Art Magazine publishers will have articles about every known religion but Christianity. It appears that it's ok to talk about Oriental philosophies, however DO NOT say anything about Christianity because it might offend someone who is not a Christian. What's with that? WELL EXCUSE ME! Self-defense that doesn't work completely sucks!

If you can win the World UFC Championship, and your the best Mixed Martial Arts fighter in the Universe, how ever when Hard times kick you in the groin, because your most valued relative died, and you just lose it and become a drunk or commit suicide you just became a victim, of not knowing beans, about self-defense. Ha! Some Champion. Hard Times development defense mentally and SPIRITUALLY. Did you know that when hard times are upon you it's no use to fight against it in your own prideful will. Instead humble yourself in the sight of the LORD, and HE will lift you up. I wished I had known that years ago when I was trying to lift myself up in the eyes of the Media. The harder I tried the more they thought I was just another wannabe trying to get free publicity. You know now that I think about it none of the other Religious sects ever promised to Guide and protect me. HUH! That is worthy of a lot of thought.

I know for sure that the Lord is faithful, and HE will establish me and GUIDE me from the evil one. Man, I like that. I feel reassured that I can count on God to be there for my stumbling clumsy self. When my hard times come, knowing the self-defense techniques to block, counter and in general ward off the attacks is the best part of my self-defense program in Keichu-Do.

Chapter Twenty-two

Kicking Against The Goads
By Steven H. Miller

I have written about this subject a bit before, but as I have studied this particular topic and how it relates to our everyday lives, I have come to realize quite a bit more and thought it was worthy of writing down and sharing.

The title of this discourse, of course, is a reference to Acts 9:5 - And he said, "Who are You, Lord?" Then the Lord said, "I am Jesus, whom you are persecuting. It [is] hard for you to kick against the goads." For years and years, I have read this verse and haven't truly understood what the significance of it is until only recently. That's what this writing is about.

In order to get a true understanding of this, you need to know what a goad is. As best as I understand it and as I have seen it defined, a goad is a long pointed stick used to drive livestock along as they are being moved from one place to another. Instead of using horses to drive the cattle, the owners use these long sticks to "goad" their cattle into going where they are needed to go. I would imagine that at some point, the cattle or other livestock get rather tired of being "goaded" and end up rebelling and not wanting to go where they are being driven. Then, unfortunately for them, the owner has to apply a bit more pressure with the goad upon the livestock's hind parts, until they comply. I again would imagine that should the rebellion continue to the point where a lot of pressure is applied, and then the livestock would end up having damage done to them. Imagine what it would be if one were to actually kick at the goad. It would indeed result in a lot of damage … eventually, if not right away.

So, thinking of all that, you can certainly see the point Jesus was making to Saul, who later became Paul, the Apostle. This incident recorded in Acts 9 is where Saul was heading to Damascus to arrest Christians and bring them back to Jerusalem for trial. By doing so, he was persecuting Jesus and was going against what God's plan was. Hence, he was kicking against the goads!

Recently, God has shown me a great deal about this particular passage of Scripture. You see, what I have discovered is that another way of kicking against the goads is to not follow God's will and direction for you life. I have come to see that many, not all but many, in the body of Christ, who are depressed, filled with anger and all sorts of other spiritual and mental maladies, are that way because they have refused to follow God's plan for their life. They are kicking against the goads and ultimately causing themselves a great deal of harm. This has become all too apparent to me, because I have spent the last several years of my life doing just that same thing and paying the price for that rebellion! So many years lost, so many opportunities not taken …

What better place for us to be than in the complete center of God's will for our lives? I think I am there now and hope to stay there the rest of my days. You say, "Yeah, but if I allow God complete control of my life and follow His plan for it, He may send me to Africa or some place like that!" SO WHAT!?!?!?! You are far better off in a small grass hut in the middle of Africa somewhere, living in the complete center of God's will for your life, than you would be living in a penthouse suite overlooking downtown Manhattan, making over $1 million a year, outside of God's will!

Why? Because in God's will for your life there is peace, there is fulfillment, there is love, there is joy, and there are things you have not yet imagined for you yet. But outside of God's will, there is nothing good for you. It is the difference between choosing blessings and curses.

Far too many of us, have bought into the lies of the devil. We have not believed what God has planted in our hearts to do. We have listened to the devil's lies of saying, "You can't do that! You're not worthy! You can't possibly believe you are called of God!" So on, so on and so forth! Blah, blah, blah! The devil will use whomever and whatever he can to keep you from becoming what God has called for you to be.

Recently, I attended revival services at a church I used to go to, and the evangelist made a statement that really stuck out at me. He said something to affect that, "If the devil has come against you and tried to make you believe that you cannot do something, it's not that he thinks you can't do it! It's that he thinks you CAN! The devil is afraid of his future and he's afraid of the fact that you ARE capable of doing what God has called you to do. It is such a great thing to know that the devil has confidence in you too!" A scary thought to be sure, but the thought of that, no the reality of that, truly hit me!

For all my life I have been told what I cannot do, what I am not possibly capable of doing. For much of the time I've been a Christian, I have had this sort of a thing too. I have had pastors, friends (so called) and others give me a list of reasons they think I cannot do what the Lord has laid upon my heart to do. They have come back time and again too. The devil has used so many of the people I had respect for to lie to me. I'm not saying all this to make you feel sorry for me or to complain. I'm telling you this so you can see the number of ways the devil will try to keep you from doing what the Lord has placed upon your heart.

Not to brag here, but I'm here to say, "No more devil! I KNOW what God has called me to do! I KNOW that I'm now headed into the complete center of God's will for my life. I KNOW that no weapon formed against me shall prosper and I KNOW that I will do my best to follow God's leading for my life or die trying."

As we all know, God loves us very much and has a special plan for our lives. Do you know what yours is? If not, I pray you begin to seek God and find out. Once you do, run with it!